FACE-TO
BIBLE STUDY SERIES

FACE-TO-FACE WITH PRISCILLA AND AQUILA

BALANCING LIFE *and* MINISTRY

Five Sessions for
Individuals, M&M'S (Mentors & Mentees), Friends, Family
or Groups

Includes

Leader's Guide for Facilitators

JANET THOMPSON

Birmingham, Alabama

New Hope® Publishers
P. O. Box 12065
Birmingham, AL 35202-2065
www.newhopepublishers.com
New Hope Publishers is a division of WMU®.

Library of Congress Cataloging-in-Publication Data

Thompson, Janet, 1947-

Face-to-face with Priscilla and Aquila : balancing life and ministry : five sessions for individuals, m&m's (mentors and mentees, friends, family) or groups : includes leader's guide for facilitators / Janet Thompson.

p. cm. -- (Face-to-face Bible study series)

Includes bibliographical references and index.

ISBN 978-1-59669-295-4 (sc : alk. paper)

1. Priscilla, Saint, 1st cent. 2. Aquila, Saint, 1st cent. 3. Christian women--Religious life--Textbooks. 4. Mentoring--Religious aspects--Christianity--Textbooks. 5. Bible--Textbooks. I. Title.

BS2520.P75T46 2011

226.6'092082--dc22

2010034530

ISBN-10: 1-59669-295-2
ISBN-13: 978-1-59669-295-4

N114132 • 0211 • 4M1

DEDICATED WITH LOVE

To

Dave, my beloved husband
and fellow worker in marriage,
work, ministry—life

TABLE OF CONTENTS

WELCOME

My Story

I began taking steps to start the Woman to Woman Mentoring Ministry while at my home church, Saddleback Church, in Lake Forest, California, pastored by Rick Warren. "Feed My sheep" was God's call and challenge to me to go into full-time ministry. God quickly revealed that *feeding* was mentoring and *the sheep* were women in churches all over the world. In obedience to the call, I launched the ministry in my home in January 1996, and we quickly outgrew my living room. After receiving numerous requests from other churches wanting to know how to start this type of a ministry, I authored *Woman to Woman Mentoring, How to Start, Grow, and Maintain A Mentoring Ministry DVD Leader Kit* (LifeWay Press).

As I traveled throughout the United States and Canada, training and speaking on mentoring, I heard numerous requests for a Bible study depicting God's plan for mentors and mentees—"M&M'S," as we fondly call them. One morning, as my husband completed his quiet time with the Lord, Dave asked me if I had ever considered writing Bible studies based on mentoring relationships in the Bible. He knew that many M&M'S enjoy doing a Bible study together, and Dave felt that one focused on what God says about mentoring relationships would help answer many of the M&M'S questions.

After much prayer—and my husband's prodding—I decided to look in the Bible to see how many mentoring relationships I could find. Before long, I had discovered 12. This was my confirmation to begin writing the "Face-to-Face" Bible study series (formerly known as *Mentoring God's Way*). My passion and life mission is to help one generation of believers connect to the next generation and pass down God's plan for the Christian life. I trust that the "Face-to-Face" Bible study series will help you do exactly that.

What Is Mentoring?

I love Dee Brestin's depiction of the informality of mentoring in *The Friendships of Women Workbook*: "It's not to be a dependent relationship, but simply a friendship as you spend time with a woman who is further down the road, at least in some areas of her Christian life. Win Couchman says, 'Mentoring works very nicely over a cup of coffee.'"

For those who like more concrete and specific definitions, *Roget's Super Thesaurus* provides this explanation of the root word of *mentoring*. It defines *mentor* as a teacher, guide, coach, or advisor. Most dictionaries define the word *mentor* as a trusted and wise counselor. To combine Dee's and the reference definitions with the Christian perspective: a Christian mentor is a spiritually mature woman who is a trusted and wise teacher, guide, coach, counselor, advisor, and friend. Thus, a *mentee* is someone willing to be taught, guided, coached, advised, or counseled by a trusted, wise, and spiritually older woman friend. Christian mentoring is sharing with another woman the many wonders you have seen God do in your life, and assuring her that He will do them in her life, too, as you both discover God's purpose and plan for your lives together.

Mentoring is not a hierarchy; it's always a two-way, mutually beneficial relationship where both participants learn from each other. Chris Tiegreen, author of my favorite devotional, *The One-Year Walk with God Devotional,* reminds us why it is always better to seek God's ways together.

> The Bible gives us solid wisdom on which to base our lives. But while it is absolute, its interpretation can vary widely. That's where advice comes in. Never underestimate the body of Christ. He has crafted us to live in community. Wisdom usually comes not to godly individuals but to godly fellowships. Are you seeking direction? Know your heart, but do not trust it entirely. Measure it by biblical wisdom and the counsel of those who follow it well. —June 27 devotional

The Bible also clearly instructs men to mentor men and women to mentor women. Titus 2:1–8 is the traditional "mentoring" passage.

> *You must teach what is in accord with sound doctrine. Teach the older men to be temperate, worthy of respect, self-controlled, and sound in faith, in love and in endurance. Likewise, teach the older women to be reverent in the way they live, not to be slanderers or*

addicted to much wine, but to teach what is good. Then they can train the younger women to love their husbands and children, to be self-controlled and pure, to be busy at home, to be kind, and to be subject to their husbands, so that no one will malign the word of God. Similarly, encourage the young men to be self-controlled. In everything set them an example by doing what is good. In your teaching show integrity, seriousness and soundness of speech that cannot be condemned, so that those who oppose you may be ashamed because they have nothing bad to say about us.

First Peter 5:2–4 (NLT) could be addressing mentors.

Care for the flock that God has entrusted to you. Watch over it willingly, not grudgingly—not for what you will get out of it, but because you are eager to serve God. Don't lord it over the people assigned to your care, but lead them by your own good example. And when the Great Shepherd appears, you will receive a crown of never-ending glory and honor.

A mentor doesn't need to be an expert on the Bible or God, and she doesn't need to have a perfect life. If that were the case, none of us would qualify. A mentor simply needs to be willing to share her life experiences with another woman and be an example and role model of how a Christian woman does life. And how do we learn to be a godly role model? Answer: *"Remember your leaders who taught you the word of God. Think of all the good that has come from their lives, and follow the example of their faith"* (Hebrews 13:7 NLT).

Mentoring is not *doing* a ministry: It is *being* a godly woman who follows the Lord's command: *"One generation will commend your works to another; they will tell of your mighty acts"* (Psalm 145:4).

WHO ARE M&M'S?

In the Woman to Woman Mentoring Ministry, we lovingly refer to mentors and mentees as "M&M'S"—no, that's not the candy, although we always have M&M's® candy at our events. And just like the candy, there are varieties of M&M relationships—no two are the same. M&M'S may be: friends, acquaintances, family members, workers, neighbors, members of a mentoring or other ministry, team members, women with similar life experiences, or any two women who want to grow spiritually together.

M&M'S AND MORE!

The "Face-to-Face" Bible study series has a variety of applications. You can enjoy this study in these ways:

On your own

As a mentor and mentee (M&M'S) in a mentoring or discipleship relationship

Between two friends

Between two relatives

As a small or large group studying together

As a churchwide Bible study

The Bible studies offer these three types of questions:

On Your Own—questions for doing the study individually

M&M'S—questions for mentors and mentees, two friends, or relatives studying together

On Your Own and M&M'S—questions applicable to both individuals and those studying together

Groups answer all the questions, with a Leader's/Facilitator's Guide in each book.

STUDY FORMAT

There are five main sessions, comprised of five study days. Each day's study includes:

Scriptures and questions for you to study and answer

Face-to-Face Reflections—a discussion of the day's topic

Personal Parable—a story depicting and applying the day's topic
Mentoring Moment—takeaway wisdom for the day

At the end of each session there is:
Faith in Action—an opportunity for life application of the lessons learned
Let's Pray Together—my prayer of agreement with you

Following session five are Closing Materials:

- Let's Pray a Closing Prayer Together
- Janet's Suggestions—ideas for further study
- Leader's Guide for Group-Study Facilitators and M&M'S
- Session Guide
- Prayer & Praise Journal

SUGGESTIONS FOR INDIVIDUAL STUDY

I admire you for seeking out this study on your own and having the desire and discipline to work on it by yourself. I like to grow in the knowledge of the Lord and His Word and have found that my most relevant insights from God come when I seek Him by myself in a quiet place. Have fun on your own, and share with someone all you are learning.

1. A good way to stay consistent in your studying is to work a little each day, during your quiet time in the morning or evening.

2. Tell someone you have started this study, and ask him or her to keep you accountable to complete it.

SUGGESTIONS FOR M&M'S— MENTORS AND MENTEES, FRIENDS, AND RELATIVES

I hope the study of *Face-to-Face with Priscilla and Aquila: Balancing Life and Ministry* adds a new dimension to your M&M relationship.

Here are a few study tips:

1. Come to your meetings prepared to discuss your answers to the session's questions.

2. Or, you may decide to answer the questions together during your meetings.

3. If you don't live near each other, you can have phone or online discussions.

4. Remember, the questions are to enlighten and not divide; be honest and open as well as loving and kind.

SUGGESTIONS FOR GROUP STUDY

I love group studies because you get to hear other people's points of view, and lasting friendships often develop. Your meetings should be fun, informative, relevant, and applicable to group members' lives. Enjoy yourself with your fellow sisters in Christ, but remember that joining a group study *does* mean commitment. So please attend your scheduled meetings unless there is a real emergency. I suggest the following courtesies:

1. Put the meeting dates on your calendar.

2. Commit to doing your study and come prepared for the discussion. This honors the rest of the group, and you will get so much more from the sessions.

3. Ask questions—quite often, someone else has the same question.

4. Participate in the discussion, but be cautious of dominating the conversation. For example, if you have answered several questions, even though you know all the answers, let someone else have a turn. Try to encourage a less outgoing member to share.

5. Listen when others speak and give each speaker your full attention.

6. Arrive on time.

7. Keep in confidence the information shared in the group.

LEADERS AND FACILITATORS

When I lead and facilitate Bible-study groups, I value a complete and detailed Leader's Guide, so that is what I have provided for you. The "Face-to-Face" Bible study series has a Leader's Guide at the end of each book to provide the leader/facilitator with creative ideas for the following:

1. Guiding group discussion

2. Adding life application and variety to the sessions

3. Accommodating the varied learning styles of the group (visual learners, hands-on learners, auditory learners, and more)

TO YOU–THE READER

Whatever way you are doing this study, God has a message and a lesson just for you. Here are some suggestions I pray will enhance your experience studying *Face-to-Face with Priscilla and Aquila.*

1. Start each session with prayer and ask the Lord to speak to you through the Scripture readings, the prayerful answering of the questions, and the interaction with others.

2. Set your own pace. I provide breaking points, but make it comfortable for yourself and break as you need to do so.

3. If you're not sure how to answer a question, move on, but continue praying and thinking about the answer. Often my answers come quickly, but God's answers are the most fruitful.

4. Unless otherwise indicated, all the questions relate to NIV Bible passages. Lists of Scriptures are sequential, as they appear in the Bible. You will be looking up Scripture references in your Bible—an invaluable way to study and learn about the Bible.

5. Use the space provided to answer questions, but don't feel obligated to fill the space. However, if you need more room, continue answering in a separate journal.

6. A book effectively used for study should be underlined, highlighted, and comments written in the margins, so interact with this material in that way.

7. At the end of session five, you will find suggestions from me on books to read or activities, to delve deeper into what God may be teaching you about the biblical M&M relationship featured in *Priscilla and Aquila*.

8. Use the Prayer & Praise Journal starting on page 138 to record the mighty work God does in your life during this study. Journal prayer requests, and note when God answers.

9. Have some chocolate. After reading about M&M'S throughout the study, you'll be ready for some candy!

My heart, admiration, and encouragement go out to you with this book. I pray that mentoring becomes a vital part of your life. The "Face-to-Face" Bible study series is another way the Lord allows me to "feed My sheep." And I hope that you will enjoy this and other "Face-to-Face" Bible studies and "feed" others as well.

About His Work,
Janet

SESSION ONE
FACE-TO-FACE WITH PRISCILLA AND AQUILA: BALANCING LIFE AND MINISTRY

THEIR STORY

Can You Relate?

William Booth and Catherine Mumford were married in June of 1885. As newlyweds, they were out in the streets preaching, teaching, and praying among the poor and needy in London, England. They believed that to save people from evil and teach them about Christ, they needed to do more than just feed and house them. So, they formed a mission and organized it as if they were in battle against the enemy. Their leaders were known as 'officers,' Christians were 'captives,' and outreaches into new cities or countries were called 'invasions.' We know this organization as the Salvation Army.

"While raising eight children, and with no one place to call home, Catherine and William were a ministry team that few can surpass. Catherine was beside her husband in every aspect of the work, helping to forge this 'army' into the militant and triumphant Christian force it has become today.

"She designed the women's uniform, including the 'Hallelujah' bonnet, and she preached the message of salvation to crowds. When she died of cancer in her sixties, it took five days for 50,000 persons to file past her casket in London's Congress Hall where she lay in state wearing her bonnet, tunic and blouse, with her Bible in her hand and her flag by her side.

"William lived twenty-two more years, continuing the ministry of the Salvation Army. Before he died, he had traveled around the world and preached 60,000 sermons. Not only have hundreds of thousands been ministered to in food and housing and in other practical ways, but, through this couple working together in service to the Lord, many thousands will live eternally in heaven with the Lord Jesus Christ."—Sylvia Charles, *Couples in the Bible*

Day One

How Does Priscilla and Aquila's Story Relate to Us?

Priscilla and Aquila are role models for balancing marriage, work, and ministry.

On Your Own and M&M's

Q: Read Priscilla and Aquila's story: Acts 18:2–3, 18–28; Romans 16:3–5*a*; 1 Corinthians 16:19; 2 Timothy 4:19. Identify their

- Work
- Ministry
- Mentoring

Q: If you're married, what would you like to learn from this study about serving as a couple?

Q: If you're not married, how do you hope to apply what you learn to your personal ministry?

M&M's

Q: Ask God to help you apply principles in this study to your M&M relationship.

Face-to-Face Reflections

As a married couple, Priscilla and Aquila worked together making a living and ministered together changing lives. They were humble tentmakers colaboring with Paul in ministry and in work and remained friends with him throughout his lifetime.

This study explores principles we can learn from this couple that are applicable to anyone wanting to learn God's plan for balancing life and ministry.

Personal Parable

The late Pastor Ray Ortlund and his wife, Anne, were a modern-day Priscilla and Aquila. Ray was a senior pastor in churches of various sizes and locations and Anne ministered beside him. As a couple, they formed Renewal Ministries and devoted their senior years to individually mentoring groups of men and women, and together mentoring couples serving in ministry. The majority of the mentoring and counseling took place in their home, and I had the privilege of participating in one of Anne's mentoring groups.

Until Ray's death, Ray and Anne traveled wherever God called them to serve, including the underground church in China when they were both well beyond getting a senior discount!

Anne, author of *Disciplines of a Beautiful Woman,* continued Renewal Ministries on her own for several years before passing the torch to their son. Like Ray, Anne seems determined to serve the Lord until she takes her final breath.

Mentoring Moment

"One man or woman called to God is worth a hundred who have elected to work for God."—Oswald Chambers

Day Two

Priscilla and Aquila Meet Their Mentor

It's not surprising that a friendship developed between the Apostle Paul and his contemporaries, Priscilla and Aquila.

On Your Own and M&M's

Q: Where did Priscilla and Aquila first meet Paul (Acts 18:1–2)?

- What nationality were Priscilla, Aquila, and Paul (Acts 18:2; 21:39)?

- What was their shared trade (Acts 18:3)?

- Why did Priscilla and Aquila leave Rome (Acts 18:2)?

- How was Paul treated in Athens, before traveling to Corinth (Acts 17:17–18, 32*a*)?

Q: How might commonalities help Paul locate Priscilla and Aquila in Corinth, a city of more than 200,000 people known for immorality and worship of the goddess Aphrodite?

Q: Describe a time when you were new in an area and trying to locate people with whom you had something in common.

Q: If you work outside the home, have you met fellow Christians at your workplace? Has being Christians in the same profession formed a bond or friendship? Explain why or why not.

Q: If you work in the home, where have you met people who share your faith and interests?

M&M'S

Q: What commonalities do you share, and how have they helped you bond?

- If you can't think of any, who is "the one" you have in common and how can you build from there?

Face-to-Face Reflections

Jewish Aquila and his wife, Priscilla, had to leave Rome when Emperor Claudius expelled all Jews—possibly, because the Jews disagreed among themselves regarding Christ as the Messiah. Commentators agree that the couple believed in Jesus and became Christians in Rome before moving to Corinth and establishing a new home and tentmaking business.

When Paul arrived in the large, thriving, pagan city of Corinth, he had just left Athens, where he faced opposition to his Christian message. Luke, the author of Acts, mentions Paul meeting Priscilla and Aquila as Paul's first significant experience upon arriving in Corinth. Jewish Christians probably congregated together in a section of the city, much like ethnic groups do today in large cities, which would help the couple and Paul meet. The three of them shared ethnicity, exile, rejection, relocation, profession, and most importantly, Jesus: a basis for a long and fruitful friendship, ministry, and working relationship.

Personal Parable

When I attend Christian writers conferences, I always make new friends because I'm among fellow authors who understand the unique trade of writing, and more importantly, who love Jesus like I do. Often, I've roomed with women I've never met, but there's an instant connection because we share commonalities that others don't usually appreciate. Paul must have felt the same when he was new in town and learned that fellow Jewish Christian tentmakers lived there.

• • •

Mentoring Moment

"Life's best revelations flash upon us while we abide in the fields of duty. Keep to your daily breadwinning and amid your toils you shall receive great benedictions and see glad visions . . . the shop or office or warehouse may become as the house of God. Do thy work and do it diligently: In it, thou mayest find rare soul fellowships, as did Aquila and Priscilla."

—Dinsdale T. Young, *Neglected People of the Bible*

• • •

Day Three

Tentmaking

Tentmaking, in general, refers to the activities of any Christian who, while functioning as a minister, receives little or no pay for his or her church work, and supports him or herself by additional, unrelated work. Specifically, tentmaking can also refer to a method of international Christian evangelism in which missionaries support themselves by working full time in the marketplace with their skills and education, instead of receiving financial support from a church. The term comes from the fact that the apostle Paul supported himself by making tents while living and preaching in Corinth (Acts 18:3)." — Wikipedia

On Your Own and M&M's

Q: Priscilla and Aquila shared the trade of tentmaking with Paul. What was the trade and legacy of the following men and women who shaped biblical history?

	Trade	Legacy
●	Abraham — Genesis 13:2	Genesis 15:4–6; 22:15–18
●	Jacob — Genesis 30:29; 32:4–5	Genesis 35:22–26

- Joseph—Genesis 41:38–41 Genesis 45:4–8

- David—1 Samuel 16:23; 17:15; 2 Samuel 2:4 Acts 13:22–23

- Nehemiah—Nehemiah 1:11*b* Nehemiah 2:3–5, 17

- Simon Peter—Mark 1:16 Mark 3:16–17; Acts 2:38–41

- Lydia—Acts 16:14 Acts 16:15, 40

- Luke—Colossians 4:14 Luke 1:3; Acts 1:1

Q: How did Paul support himself and his missionary journeys?

- Acts 18:3; 20:33–35
- 1 Corinthians 9:6–18
- 2 Corinthians 11:7–9
- 1 Thessalonians 2:9
- 2 Thessalonians 3:7–10

Q: Read Philippians 4:14–19. How did Paul receive offers of financial support?

Q: Do you know a "tentmaker" who supports his or her ministry by working outside the ministry or by donations? Explain.

- What motivates people to serve unpaid?

Q: Are you a "tentmaker" or could you imagine yourself in that position? Why or why not?

Q: Write your thoughts on working to support ministry instead of lifestyle.

- How is this countercultural?

- How could this practice apply to your life?

Q: List ways, other than monetary, of contributing to a ministry.

Q: Locate "tentmakers" in your church or community and offer assistance.
- If you can't identify tentmakers, how could you assist missionaries your church supports?

- Journal and share with others the results and rewards of this experience.

M&M's

Q: Together help a "tentmaker" or missionary.
Q: Identify a ministry you could work in together—consider serving in a mentoring ministry.

Face-to-Face Reflections

Paul sought work as a master tentmaker or leather worker to support himself while pursuing his main purpose—the ministry of spreading the gospel. Like the skilled biblical characters you studied, Paul's profession is not his legacy.

Today, many people feel secular careers *are* their main purpose and legacy, with ministry relegated to "spare time." Others feel their sole purpose in life is furthering the kingdom and only work to pay the bills and support their ministry. Then there are those whose work is their ministry. Never confuse a career with significance.

Personal Parable

My husband and I are tentmakers. I quit my career to found and lead the Woman to Woman Mentoring Ministry. Our plan was for my husband to support us financially with his lucrative career, while I served in full-time ministry. Three months after leaving my paying job, Dave was part of a corporate layoff and out of work for 18 months. During that time, Woman to Woman Mentoring grew rapidly, and we self-published the first *Woman to Woman Mentoring How to Start, Grow, and Maintain a Mentoring Ministry Kit*. By faith we invested in the kit and prayed for God's provision.

Friends and family became concerned that we weren't working and began asking, "When is Janet going back to work?" Dave would respond, "Janet *is* working. She's about the Lord's work." Thus, my speaking and writing ministry became About His Work Ministries.

After several short-lived jobs, Dave eventually secured labor-intensive work with an extermination company. He also served at our church as a couples' small-group community leader. Together we "make tents" to pay the bills, so God can use us where He wills.

• • •

Mentoring Moment

William Carey was a shoe cobbler accused of neglecting his business because of his ministerial efforts. His response was, "Neglecting my business? My business is to extend the Kingdom of God. I only cobble shoes to pay expenses."

• • •

Day Four

Priscilla and Aquila Mentor a Mentee

Imagine listening to a learned scholar, pastor, or teacher and suddenly you notice he or she omits an important piece of information. What do you do?

On Your Own and M&M's

Q: What did Priscilla and Aquila do in this situation (Acts 18:24–26)?

- What was wise about how they handled the incident?
- How did their intervention benefit Apollos?
- How did it benefit Apollos' audiences (Acts 18:27–28)?

Q: Why is misinformed or misguided zeal dangerous?

- Proverbs 19:2
- Romans 10:1–4
- Galatians 4:17–18

Q: How are we to channel our spiritual enthusiasm (Romans 12:11)?

Q: Have you been in a similar situation as Priscilla and Aquila?

- What did you do?

- Would you do anything differently now?

M&M's

Q: Mentor, your mentee may say or do inappropriate things. How can you honor her enthusiasm while mentoring her?

- Mentee, if you're a new Christian, don't allow lacking all the facts dampen your zeal for sharing the good news, but also be an eager learner.

Q: Apollos was more educated and esteemed than his mentors. If this is the case in your M&M relationship, how are you dealing with any awkwardness?

Face-to-Face Reflections

Apollos's message was not inaccurate or insincere; it was simply incomplete. As an educated Jew, he was knowledgeable in the Old Testament and boldly taught from it in the synagogue, but he lacked teaching on the full gospel story. Often, ardently enthusiastic new believers feel immediately ready to teach in the church, or even be a mentor. They may not realize that they're babes in Christ with a conversion experience and testimony, but in need of teaching, discipling, training, and maturing in the Word. It takes grace and tact to correct without squelching zeal.

Apollos came from cosmopolitan Alexandria, the second most important city in the Roman Empire and a center for education and philosophy, touting a university and library. Priscilla and Aquila were tentmakers. Occasionally, a mentee will be more highly educated and maybe even older than the mentor, but the mentor is spiritually older and more mature in his or her faith. This may seem backwards when measured by the world's standards of success and achievement, and the M&M'S could require a time of adjustment, but it didn't seem to bother Apollos. He was an eager student and a quick learner.

Personal Parable

Dave and I mentored our daughter Kim and her husband, Toby, when they were new believers. While studying the Book of Genesis, Kim exclaimed, "Oh, that's who Abraham is! When I was in preschool and we sang about Abraham and all his children, I thought we were singing about Abraham Lincoln!" Another time she asked if we were going to study from the First or Second Testament. We had a good chuckle as Kim good-naturedly accepted clarification.

However, she took a class at church and her worse fear came true when they asked everyone to share their favorite Bible story. She didn't have any favorites yet because she was just starting to read the Bible. She wanted to crawl under the table. We'll talk more in session four about mentoring and discipling new believers; but remember, no matter how much you know now, once you too were a babe in Christ.

• • •

Mentoring Moment

"If a man is called to preach the Gospel, God will crush him till the light of the eye, the power of the life, the ambition of the heart, is all riveted on Himself. That is not done easily. It is not a question of saintliness, it has to do with the Call of God."

—Oswald Chambers

• • •

Day Five

Where God Leads, We Will Go

In *Lectures to My Students*, the nineteenth-century preacher, Charles Spurgeon, defines "the call" to ministry: "The first sign of the heavenly calling is an intense, all-absorbing desire for the work. In order to be a true call to the ministry there must be an irresistible, overwhelming craving and raging thirst for telling to others what God has done to our own souls."

On Your Own and M&M's

Q: Paul was a missionary committed to travel where God led, but why do you think Priscilla and Aquila followed Paul from Corinth to Ephesus, a 300-mile boat trip (Acts 18:18–19)?

- What purpose did God have (Acts 18:24–26)?

Q: Use these Scriptures to trace Priscilla and Aquila's travel timeline and how God used them in each new place.

	Location	Ministry
Acts 18:1–3		
Acts 18:18–19, 24–26; 1 Corinthians 16:19		
Romans 1:7; 16:3–5		
2 Timothy 4:19		

Q: How did their willingness to move help the church?

- What would each move require to establish their business and home?

Q: Priscilla and Aquila's mentor, Paul, often spoke of the Holy Spirit guiding his travels (Acts 16:8; 20:22–24). How might this have influenced the couple's receptiveness to relocate (Isaiah 6:8)?

Q: God often requires a physical move to follow His plan. Identify: Person/People Called? Did they initially follow God's call? How did God bless them?

Genesis 6:12–21	Genesis 6:22	Genesis 9:1
Genesis 12:1	Genesis 12:4–5	Genesis 12:2–3
Exodus 4:19	Exodus 4:20	Deuteronomy 34:10–12
Exodus 6:6–8	Exodus 6:9	Exodus 3:8
Jonah 1:1	Jonah 1:3	Jonah 3:1–5
Matthew 2:19	Matthew 2:21–22	Matthew 2:23

Q: Following God's call also may involve taking a risk. Speculate Priscilla and Aquila's risks in moving and befriending Paul (Acts 17:1–9; Romans 16:3–4).

- What risks have you taken to follow God's call?

Q: God doesn't always require a move, but what changes in life-style might be involved?

Q: Has God asked you to move or make a change to follow Him? Did you do it willingly or resist? Explain.

On Your Own

Q: What "calling" has God put on your heart and what would it require?

M&M'S

Q: Did following the call to be an M&M require any significant changes?

Q: Discuss how you can support each other in making changes that would allow more ministry involvement.

Face-to-Face Reflections

Priscilla and Aquila willingly moved their home and business every three to five years to further the cause of Christ. Historians place them married and living in Rome for ten years before their exile to Corinth, where they lived for three years. Paul lived with them for the last 18 months and the church probably started in their home.

Then the couple packed up and sailed with Paul to Ephesus. When Paul left for Syria, Priscilla and Aquila stayed on for three years carrying on Paul's ministry while the church met in their home.

When a new emperor arose in Rome, the Jewish expulsion edict of Claudius elapsed and Priscilla and Aquila returned to Rome. They either started a new church there or picked up the ministry they had ten years earlier, before their exile. Five years later, the couple returned to Ephesus to minister with the timid young pastor, Timothy (2 Timothy 1:2, 7), who surely welcomed the support and encouragement of this spiritually seasoned couple.

Both spouses must have "the calling" to minister as a couple. Maybe it won't be full-time ministry, but perhaps starting like Priscilla and Aquila by hosting a visiting pastor or Bible study.

Personal Parable

I heard God's call to "Feed My sheep" when I had a family at home, a full-time career, and was attending seminary. I had no idea who the sheep were or how I would feed them, but through a series of "God-incidences," the Lord revealed that feeding was mentoring, and the sheep were women in the church.

Following God's call has required drastic changes and risks, but my husband was on board with my calling and felt his calling was to provide support and encouragement for "our ministry." We went from being financially secure and living comfortably to living frugally, but oh so rich in blessings.

Mentoring Moment

"Many preachers are good tailors spoiled, and capital shoemakers turned out of their proper calling. When God means a creature to fly, He gives it wings; and when He intends men to preach, He gives them abilities."—Charles Spurgeon

Faith in Action

What one thing from this session does God want you to apply in your life today?

Let's Pray Together

Lord, we want to be committed to go where You lead. Give us discernment and wisdom to hear and respond to Your still small voice. Remove any barriers, fears, or anxiety involved in following Your call. For those of us who are married, help us remain united in purpose and in deed. If it isn't the season of life for us to serve full-time in ministry, encourage us to support the efforts of those who are spreading the good news. Help us be faithful in all we do for You. Amen.

SESSION TWO
FACE-TO-FACE WITH PRISCILLA AND AQUILA: BALANCING LIFE AND MINISTRY

Maturing in Faith Together

Day One

Partners in Faith

Faith is personal, but for married couples and business partners like Priscilla and Aquila, shared faith is essential.

On Your Own and M&M's

Q: How do we acquire personal faith (John 3:16; 1 John 1:9)?

Q: Second Corinthians 1:24 (*The Message*) reads: *"We're not in charge of how you live out the faith, looking over your shoulders, suspiciously critical. We're partners, working alongside you, joyfully expectant. I know that you stand by your own faith, not by ours."* Explain the relationship of personal to shared faith.

- How could personal faith lead to shared faith?

Q: Why is shared faith important in partnerships (2 Corinthians 6:14)?

- 2 Corinthians 6:14 (*The Message*) defines "yoked together" as *partners with*. What areas of life could this apply to?

- How can you determine if someone shares your faith?

Q: How could an unbelieving spouse be positively influenced (1 Peter 3:1–2)?

- Apply this concept to other unequally yoked relationships.

Q: Not partnering with an unbeliever doesn't mean we can't be friends or acquaintances, but what do Jeremiah 15:19*b* and John 17:15–16 warn?

Q: If you're not married, why is it essential to date Christians?

On Your Own

Q: Whom could you partner in faith with to work for God?

M&M's

Q: Do you both share the same personal faith?

Q: Mentee, if you don't have a personal relationship with Jesus Christ, what is holding you back from making that decision? Discuss those issues with your mentor.

- If you're ready to accept Jesus into your heart, pray the salvation prayer on page 37. You can pray it on your own, but your mentor would love to share this experience with you.

Q: How might God use your shared faith to partner together in working for Him? Brainstorm ideas of projects you could do together.

Salvation Prayer

Dear Jesus, I know that I have sinned in my life, and I want to tell You how sorry I am. I ask You now to forgive me and cleanse me of those sins. Jesus, I want You to come into my heart and take residence there. I believe You are the Son of God and that You died on the Cross to pay the price for my sins and then rose again in three days to offer me eternal life. Jesus, I give You complete control of my life, and I willingly surrender my heart, mind, and soul to You. Please fill me with the Holy Spirit and Your love. Lord, I give You my life—make me a new creation in You. In Your Son Jesus' name, I pray. Amen.

If you prayed the salvation prayer, welcome to the family of God! God just wiped away your past sins, and you have a new slate: a new life in Christ. Congratulations! Celebrate and tell others about the decision you just made to become a follower of Jesus Christ—it's your testimony. You are ready to grow and mature spiritually in your personal faith and share that faith with others. This study will have so much more meaning to you now.

Face-to-Face Reflections

Associating with believers doesn't make us a Christian just as associating with married couples doesn't make us married. A group of couples may get married at the same time, but each couple says their own personal vows to each other, not to the group. Likewise, we might be in a group when we accept Christ as our personal Savior, but the key word is *personal*. When we make our own profession of faith in Jesus, we share the same faith as the believing group.

Once you have a personal faith, you can further the cause of Christ by teaming up with others who share your faith: a spouse, friends, relatives, co-workers, ministries, small groups...an M&M.

Personal Parable

In my book *Praying for Your Prodigal Daughter*, my daughter Kim explains that even though she was living a wayward lifestyle and hadn't accepted Jesus as her personal Savior, she thought that because her family was Christian, she was automatically a Christian too. Dave and I gave Kim and her fiancé, Toby, a biblically based premarital course, and they both accepted a *personal* relationship with Jesus in that class. Praise God, Kim and her husband are "equally yoked." Here is an excerpt from Kim's testimony in the book.

> Pastor Pete made it clear we couldn't get to heaven on our parents' faith—something I really thought I could count on—it had to be our own personal decision and relationship with Christ. That really got us to thinking. I know that because we committed our lives to Christ, God has blessed our marriage.

• • •

Mentoring Moment

Sitting in church doesn't make you a Christian anymore than sitting in a garage makes you a car.

• • •

Day Two

Studying God's Word

As Jews, Priscilla and Aquila would have studied the Torah, but they also lived during the era of the New Testament and the divinely inspired letters of Paul.

On Your Own and M&M's

Q: Paul sent greetings to, or from, Priscilla and Aquila in his letters to the Romans, Corinthians, and Ephesians, so we assume the couple read the letters. What would Priscilla and Aquila learn from Paul regarding the value of studying the Scriptures?

- Acts 17:2, 10–12
- Romans 1:1–3
- Romans 10:10–11
- Romans 15:3–4
- 1 Corinthians 15:3–5
- 2 Timothy 2:8–10

Q: Read John 1:1–4. Who was the Incarnation of God's Word?

Q: What does Jesus compare Himself to in John 6:48–51?

- Why does Jesus use food as an analogy?
- What happens to physical life without food?

Q: Explain the prognosis of a spiritual life starved of God's Word.

- Are you starving or feasting on God's Word?

Q: How might Lamentations 3:23 inspire you to read the Bible daily?

- Variety in food is enjoyable; how could you add variety to ingesting God's Word?

On Your Own

Q: List benefits of studying God's Word with someone or in a small group.

M&M's

Q: Discuss the value of doing this Bible study together.

Face-to-Face Reflections

Studying God's Word together is like savoring a delicious meal with someone rather than eating alone. If you're doing this study on your own, I commend you for taking the time and having the discipline, and I'm sure you're receiving a blessing. But consider that bouncing ideas off another person, or listening to someone else's interpretation of a Scripture, broadens understanding and application. Conversely, God may have revealed something to you in reading His Word that He wants shared with others.

Whether you prefer studying on your own or in a group, it's an undisputed fact that you cannot spiritually grow and mature without consistently studying God's Word.

Personal Parable

My husband and I met in a small-group Bible study that he was coleading. Having recently rededicated my life, I knew I needed to study God's Word. I didn't *know* my Bible the way I wanted to *know* my Lord. Our pastor, Rick Warren, tells the church repeatedly that we are "better together" in small groups, so I took his challenge and received a double blessing!

After we were married, Dave and I led Bible study groups together, and separately, and our newly blended family studied the Bible together to know God, and each other, better. Dave and I continue studying our Bible together and individually, a practice that has grown our faith and our marriage.

Mentoring Moment

"It is a wonderful thing.... It is glorious to be so far out on the ocean of divine love, believing in God, and steering for heaven straight away, by the direction of the Word of God."
—Charles Spurgeon

Day Three

Praying Continuously

Wherever Priscilla and Aquila lived, their home was the meeting place for the church. Their living room was the scene for many prayers, praises, and strengthened faith.

On Your Own and M&M's

Q: Read Acts 1:13–15. What was the first thing the disciples and believers did after Jesus' ascension?

- How often did they pray (v. 14)?

- How did they grow in faith (Acts 2:42–47)?

Q: Read the believers' prayer in Acts 4:23–31. What were they praying in verses 25–26?

- What was the result of their prayers (v. 31)?

- Experience praying Scripture by personalizing and praying their prayer aloud.

Q: By each Scripture below, note how Priscilla and Aquila might have applied mentor Paul's wisdom regarding prayer. How could you apply it?

	PRISCILLA AND AQUILA	YOU
Romans 1:8–11		
Romans 12:12		
Ephesians 6:10–20		
1 Thessalonians 5:17		

Q: What is an important element of prayer (Psalm 134:1)?

- Why is praise vital to faith?
- Who benefits from praise?

Q: What are the benefits of praying with someone (Matthew 18:19–20)?

- List reasons people might feel uncomfortable praying together.

- What is the root of the reasons you've listed?

- What is the antidote (1 John 4:18)?

Q: If you're married, do you pray together? Why or why not?

- If you do, how has this grown your faith and marriage?

Q: Record your prayers and God's replies in the Prayer & Praise Journal at the end of the book.

On You Own

Q: In what ways would a prayer partner be valuable?

M&M's

Q: Mentor, open and close meetings in prayer and journal prayer requests and praises.

Q: Mentee, participate in times of prayer. Start by prayerfully reading your prayer requests.

Q: How does praying and praising together strengthen your faith?

Face-to-Face Reflections

Praying together is an integral component of any Christian relationship, yet many married couples—including pastors and their wives—admit seldom, if ever, praying together. Reasons given:

feel self-conscious and vulnerable, don't know what to say, won't sound spiritual enough—fear. Mentees have many of the same concerns about praying openly with their mentor and some small group participants shy away from participating in prayertime.

In the leader's guide on pages 122–24, there are suggestions for group prayer. Rather than focusing on your spouse, mentor, small-group members, or others in the room, speak to God as someone you love, who also loves you.

Personal Parable

My husband and I pray together daily, and we can attest to the power of praying as a couple. In the morning, we pray for each other's day and any requests God puts on either of our hearts. In the evening, we thank Him for another day of life. When we're apart, we pray together on the phone. Satan might have a heyday with our lives and ministry if we didn't unite as one in prayer—but we don't give him the opportunity.

• • •

Mentoring Moment

"The one concern of the devil is to keep Christians from praying. He fears nothing from prayerless studies, prayerless work, prayerless religion. He laughs at our toil, mocks at our wisdom, but trembles when we pray." —Samuel Chadwick

• • •

Day Four

Remaining Christ-Centered

God works mightily through a couple devoted to Christ and willing to use their time, energy, efforts, talents, and resources to further the kingdom.

On Your Own and M&M's

Q: Compare Priscilla and Aquila's marriage with that of Sapphira and Ananias (Acts 5:1–11).

- How did each couple unite in purpose?

- Who was at the center of their efforts?

- Compare Priscilla and Aquila's sharing with the other couple's hoarding (Luke 16:13).

- What was the outcome of both couple's lives?

Q: Hebrews 3:1–2 in *The Message* defines Christ-centeredness: *"So, my dear Christian friends, companions in following this call to the heights, take a good hard look at Jesus. He's the centerpiece of everything we believe, faithful in everything God gave him to do."* How do you personally remain Christ-centered?

- Define a Christ-centered relationship and how to maintain it.

Q: List ways a Christ-centered marriage is a role model for other married couples.

- How is a Christ-centered business partnership a role model for other business owners?

Q: If you have an unbelieving spouse or business partner, what obstacles do you have to overcome to maintain a Christ-centered life?

- How is your life a witness to the unbeliever?

On Your Own

Q: How do you maintain Christ-centered relationships?

M&M's

Q: Mentor, share with your mentee ways she can maintain Christ-centered relationships.

Face-to-Face Reflections

The Soul Care Bible personality profile for Priscilla and Aquila describes their marriage:

A Christ-centered home can be a haven for many who need to hear the gospel message. A devoted couple can minister together to both men and women. As they seek God together, their united front and solid faith can be a positive example to many.

Personal Parable

Read how a couple maintains a Christ-centered marriage, even when apart:

> Sharon and I have different ministries that often take us in opposite directions, though we do our best to connect to each other's ministries. But to maintain our togetherness as a couple bound together, not just by our own love but also by the love of God in Christ, we have developed a shared daily spiritual discipline...."Celtic Daily Prayer"...daily liturgies and two annual cycles of readings, drawing both from ancient Celtic Christian writings and stories as well as contemporary Christian writings and witness. Whether we are together or apart (I travel a lot as an IM global missionary), we share this daily discipline of liturgy readings and prayers. It has become a key part of our spiritual rhythm and strength as a couple.
> —Dan Buttry, "Priscilla and Aquila Network Bulletin Board," May 19, 2006

• • •

Mentoring Moment

The closer you each grow to Christ,
the closer you grow to each other.

• • •

Day Five

Sharing Your Testimony

Priscilla and Aquila shared their faith with others. Our willingness to share our testimony of becoming a believer could help others make the same decision for Christ.

On Your Own and M&M's

Q: What is a testimony (Psalm 105:1–3; 1 John 5:11)?

Q: What does Paul pray that another couple's house church will share (Philemon 2, 4–7)?

Q: What can you learn from these testimonies?

	Person	Testimony	How Received
John 1:18–34; 3:32			

Person	Testimony	How Received
John 4:39–42		
John 5:36–37; 8:12–30		
John 9:1–41		
Acts 26:1–32		

Q: Why does God want us to share our personal testimonies (1 Corinthians 1:5–7)?

Q: How do Paul's inadequacies in 1 Corinthians 2:1–5 encourage you to share your testimony?

Q: Read 1 Peter 3:14–16. Will you share the reason for your hope, even if it isn't appreciated? Why or why not?

On Your Own

Q: Q Have you shared your personal testimony? If not, pray for an opportunity and a willingness to tell what God has done in your life.

M&M's

Q: Tell each other your personal testimony of Christ changing your life.

Q: How can your relationship be a testimony?

- Make a commitment to find a venue to share your testimony together.

Face-to-Face Reflections

Not everyone wants to hear our testimony. Many will rebuff us, like those you studied today; but like them, we cannot let rejection stop us from sharing the way Christ changed our life and is our source of hope. God wants to use our story to change other people's lives too.

You never know when the opportunity will arise to give your testimony, so be prepared. In his book, *The Purpose Driven Life*, Pastor Rick Warren suggests writing out your testimony first and dividing it into four parts:

1. What my life was like before I met Jesus
2. How I realized I needed Jesus
3. How I committed my life to Jesus
4. The difference Jesus has made in my life

Personal Parable

I share my testimony when I speak and my story runs through my writings. Sometimes I give a long version, or I shorten it when time or space is limited. One day a friend, who often spoke with me, commented that my testimony always sounded the same. I told her to worry if it ever changed. We shouldn't tire of telling the wonders we have seen God do, or add anything for dramatic effect. "Once I was blind, but now I see," is sufficiently dramatic!

Mentoring Moment

The key to making your story your testimony is focusing on God and not yourself. Don't dramatize how bad you were: characterize how good God is!

Faith in Action

What one thing from this session does God want you to apply in your life today?

Let's Pray Together

Lord, help us to hunger and thirst for Your Word. Never let us tire of reading Your promises and instructions for living our life. Keep us ready to hear the promptings of the Holy Spirit and to stay in continual communication with You through prayer. Let our lives so shine for You that others will believe. Keep our marriages strong in faith and protect us from the enemy who would try to destroy our relationships and our witness. Keep us humble, Lord, never thinking that we have arrived in spiritual knowledge, but always ready to share with others what Your Word and Your ways have taught us. In Jesus' name we pray, amen.

SESSION THREE
FACE-TO-FACE WITH PRISCILLA AND AQUILA: BALANCING LIFE AND MINISTRY

SERVING TOGETHER

Day One

An Open Heart and Home

Priscilla and Aquila understood that teaching, worshipping, evangelizing, fellowshipping, and maturing in faith requires community. In spite of frequent moves, Priscilla and Aquila's home was a safe and welcoming place for believers to assemble.

On Your Own and M&M's

Q: How did Priscilla and Aquila open their home and heart to Paul (Acts 18:3)?

Q: Where did the first church meet and worship (Acts 5:42; 20:20)?

- What took place in homes (Acts 2:42, 46–47)?

- Besides housing Paul, how did Priscilla and Aquila use their home (Acts 18:26; Romans 16:3–5; 1 Corinthians 16:19)?

Q: Who else opened their heart and homes to Paul and the church (Acts 16:13–15, 40; Philemon 2, 22)?

Q: When Jesus sent the disciples out to minister, where did He tell them to stay (Mark 6:10)?

Q: List excuses Priscilla could have used to discourage church meetings at her home.

- Have you used any of these or do you enjoy hosting church functions?

Q: Picture this scenario: You've worked all day and hurriedly left a messy house to go to church to hear a guest speaker. Suddenly, it's apparent the speaker needs discipling, and your husband invites him to *your* house tonight for a chat! Circle responses that would apply to you.

Wait until I get my husband alone!
The house is a wreck.
Our home isn't worthy.
I don't have cookies or tea.
I'm exhausted.
It's too late.
We have to get up early.
We were there for a reason.
Who are we to disciple a scholar?
God wants *us* to talk to the teacher.
He will feel more comfortable in our home.
Let's talk to him outside the church.
If one of these didn't fit you, fill in the blank______________.

Q: How do these verses challenge you?

- Romans 12:13

- 1 Peter 4:9

- 3 John 5–8

Q: How often is your answer, "Not now, Lord"? Explain.

Q: Think outside the box and list ways Christians can use their homes for ministry.

- Have you done any of these? Why or why not?

- If yes, describe the experience.

- If not, which one would you consider trying?

M&M'S

Q: If you meet in one of your homes, you're ministering there. What other ways could you use your homes for God's glory?

Q: Plan a ministry project that would center in one of your homes.

Face-to-Face Reflections

The new church met for corporate worship outdoors in the temple courts. But after corporate worship, they dispersed among each other's homes for food, fellowship, the Lord's Supper, prayer, and more teaching. It wasn't until the end of the third century that the Christian church began holding corporate worship in church buildings. Today, many churches pattern after the early church with weekend corporate worship services in a building and small- or cell-group Bible studies in homes during the week.

Mans Ramstad, involved in a "tentmaking ministry" with his family in an Asian country, stresses the significance of worshipping in homes on the missions field: "This good example of Priscilla and Aquila shows the role of the home in ministry. In many of the countries we live in, we are not allowed to evangelize and preach publicly, but we have tremendous freedom in what we do with individuals or small groups of people in our homes."

PERSONAL PARABLE

When the Woman to Woman Mentoring Ministry was in the planning stages, I felt the Lord guiding me to hold Orientation Coffees in homes for the prospective M&M'S to meet, and the first coffee should be in my home! I wrestled with the Lord, protesting that my home was too small, my couch too old and ugly, and wallpaper was peeling off the guest bathroom wall—projects planned for after our last child left home in March, but the coffee was in January.

I objected, "Lord, women can't come into my house with it looking like this." His response was, *When the beautiful women sit on your couch, all that will be visible is their smiling radiant faces. Their loveliness will cover the stains and tatters.* Then He gave me the idea to tape the bathroom's peeling wallpaper, remove the lightbulbs, and use candles.

I'm so glad I didn't let my perfectionism stop me from having that first coffee at my home, because little did I know it would be the first of thousands of Woman to Woman Mentoring Ministry orientation coffees held in homes around the world.

• • •

Mentoring Moment

"Every home can transform itself into a little church. Not only in the sense that in them must reign the typical Christian love made of altruism and of reciprocal care, but still more in the sense that the whole of family life, based on faith, is called to revolve around the singular lordship of Jesus Christ."—Benedict XVI

• • •

Day Two

Lay Ministering

"The ministry of the laity is 'to represent Christ and his Church; to bear witness to him wherever they may be; and, according to the gifts given them, to carry on Christ's work of reconciliation in the world; and to take their place in the life, worship, and governance of the Church' (*The Book of Common Prayer*). Much of the ministry of the laity thus takes place outside official church structures in homes, workplaces, schools, and so forth. Laymen also play important roles in the structures of the church." —Wikipedia

On Your Own and M&M's

Q: How were Priscilla and Aquila lay ministers?

Q: Read Ephesians 2:8–10. How does this verse support the premise that each Christian has a specific ministry?

- What do you think yours is?

Q: What is *every* believer's ministry (Matthew 28:18–20)?

Q: Who set the bar for selfless, payless serving (Matthew 20:28)?

- What blessings come from serving for "free"?

- How might this be a hard concept for some to understand?

Q: Pastor Rick Warren in *The Purpose Driven Life* clarifies the term *minister*: "When most people hear 'ministry,' they think of pastors, priests, and professional clergy, but God says every member of his family is a minister. In the Bible, the words *servant* and *minister* are synonyms, as are *service* and *ministry*. If you are a Christian, you are a minister, and when you're serving, you're ministering.... Regardless of your job or career, you are called to full-time Christian service. A 'non-serving Christian' is a contradiction in terms."

- How does it feel to think of yourself as a "minister"?

- How is mentoring a ministry?

- Where do you, or could you, serve or minister?

M&M'S

Q: Mentor, how are you a lay minister as a mentor?

Q: Mentee, how can you prepare yourself to minister as a mentor?

Q: What other ways can you minister together or separately?

Face-to-Face Reflections

We aren't saved by our works—our faith results in works. When you freely serve others in the name of Jesus Christ, you're lay ministering. Life experiences plus faith equals a ministry opportunity. Vickie Kraft in *The Influential Woman* encourages women to step out in faith:

> Just for the record, let's assure ourselves that women who reach out to women don't have to be graduates of colleges, universities, seminaries, or Bible schools. You may not have a degree from anywhere. But you do have something that is much more important. You have lived! .... No matter where life has taken you, you have gone through all kinds of joy and suffering and you have something to share. Why? Because in spite of all you've been through, you have not become embittered toward God. Instead you've walked with Him. You've let Him minister to you. You have not turned away, but have instead grown closer to Him. And now you have something to offer others who are in the very same boat.

Priscilla and Aquila are examples of how lay ministers can use their hands, hearts, and homes to help further the Lord's work. Every pastor and missionary thanks God for people like Priscilla and Aquila. If you're a lay minister, somewhere someone is thanking God for you.

Personal Parable

The focus of my seminary degree is to equip the laity to minister in their lives, homes, and churches: to help them internalize that God saves each of us for a reason that goes beyond our own personal growth and maturity. In my *Woman to Woman Mentoring Ministry Coordinator's Guide*, I caution lay ministers not to think of themselves as "volunteers": "I do not use the words *volunteer* or *volunteering*. Instead, you will see the terms *helper, servant, opportunity to serve, service opportunities, offer*, or *want to serve*. When we choose to volunteer, we are often still in control. When we offer to be a servant or a helper, God is in control."

The heart of the Great Commission is for every believer to tell others the good news of Jesus Christ and equip them to go out and do the same. God wants to do extraordinary things through ordinary people. I don't need to be a pastor or on a church staff to take the Great Commission and mentoring to thousands of women all over the world, and neither do you.

• • •

Mentoring Moment

"True service comes from a relationship with the divine Other deep inside. We serve out of whispered prompting, divine urgings. Energy is expended, but it is not the frantic energy of the flesh.... True service finds it almost impossible to distinguish the small from the large service." — Richard Foster, *Celebration of Discipline*

• • •

Day Three

Fellow Workers for Christ

Priscilla and Aquila colabored together in marriage and with Paul in business and ministry. Often married couples serve separately in churches, and while their gifts are valuable in different places, they should consider impacting the kingdom together.

On Your Own and M&M'S

Q: How did Paul often refer to people who served with him in evangelistic ministry (Romans 16:3, 9; 2 Corinthians 6:1; Philippians 4:3; Colossians 4:11; Philemon 24)?

- Define the term *fellow workers*.

- How does this term eliminate hierarchy and promote unity?

- What current terms have the same meaning?

Q: How does Paul admonish the Corinthian church for their disunity (1 Corinthians 3:1–9)?

- What were they acting like (vv. 1–3)?

- Why were they quarreling (v. 4)?

- What are Apollos and Paul called (v. 5)?

- How did Paul and Apollos work together (vv. 6–7)?

- Who was responsible for their success?

- What is their common purpose (v. 8)?

- What are *all* Christians (v. 9)?

Q: In what areas could a married couple be "fellow workers"?

- If you're married, have you considered your marriage in those terms? Why or why not?

On Your Own

Q: With whom are you a fellow worker for Christ?

M&M's

Q: How could you become fellow workers for Christ?

Face-to-Face Reflections

When Paul referred to Priscilla and Aquila as *"fellow workers in Christ Jesus,"* he indicated equality—they were working side by side, whether making tents, on a missions trip, or leading the church—and so it should be in all ministry. We need each other.

The Salvation Army, and often the Bible and hymns, refer to Christians as soldiers combating an evil force. In his book, *The Art of the Leader,* William A. Cohen draws on his military background to explain the importance of having fellow workers in the battle.

> Army historian Brigadier General S. L. A. Marshall, who conducted more than four hundred interviews with American Infantrymen immediately after combat...concluded that the main motivation for a soldier to fight is a sense of psychological unity with other members of his immediate combat unit.

Personal Parable

Early in our marriage, Dave and I trained with Gary Smalley's ministry to lead "Making Love Last Forever" groups. Preparing lesson plans and leading the group as fellow workers for Christ strengthened our own marriage.

Currently, we lead a support group for parents of prodigals, taking them through *Praying for Your Prodigal Daughter.* My husband and I soldiered side by side through the prodigal child experience, and God uses us to soldier with other parents in the battle for our children's souls.

• • •

Mentoring Moment

"I hold it to be one of the simplest truths of war that the thing which enables an infantry soldier to keep going with his weapons is the near presence or presumed presence of a comrade."
—Brigadier General S. L. A. Marshall

• • •

Day Four

Allowing God to Use Your Gifts

The gifted couple, Priscilla and Aquila, could have used their talents for worldly fame and fortune, but they *chose* to serve the Lord.

On Your Own and M&M's

Q: Who is the giver of gifts (1 Corinthians 7:7)?

Q: What do these verses say about gifts and how to use them?

- Romans 12:6–8

- 1 Corinthians 12:7–10, 27–31

- 1 Peter 4:10–11

Q: Identify Priscilla and Aquila's gifts.

- How did they use their gifts to serve God?

Q: What gifts and talents has God given you to use for Him?

- How are you using them?

M&M'S

Q: How are you merging your gifts and talents to serve God?

Face-to-Face Reflections

Priscilla and Aquila were among the earliest known teachers of Christian theology, and they were a talented and gifted team skilled in working with leather, a talent used to make something people needed—tents. This business savvy probably allowed them to own a home, where they applied their gifts of hospitality, mentoring, and evangelism.

Priscilla and Aquila also had the unique gift of "letting go"—not remaining tied to any one spot. They displayed the treasured gift of loyalty as life-long friends of Paul. Their gift of discernment and timing allowed them to guide and correct Apollos, and they approached him as a team, neither taking credit for noticing the error. This couple applied the gift of unity—a great role model for any observers. What a couple!

Personal Parable

Married couple and ministry team, Karen and Robin, served together on the board of Christian Marriage Encounter. They combined their individual gifts by having Robin do administrative work and Karen relational work.

Karen tells the story of discerning that a male unbeliever in one of their groups might be ready to accept Jesus. She gently approached the subject with the man, and then Robin took over and prayed with him. This couple is a modern-day Priscilla and Aquila, who for 30 years have combined their gifts and talents to found and run a camp for abused children.

• • •

Mentoring Moment

God doesn't give you the ability to do *everything*; He does give you the aptitude to do *anything*.

• • •

Day Five

Iron Sharpening Iron

On Your Own and M&M's

"The apostle Paul was clearly a man committed to raising up a band of special friends. He knew who they were, and he regularly recognized them for their contribution to his spiritual passion. His friends were a resource upon which he obviously depended and without which he would not have survived. His address book for special friends would have included Aquila and Priscilla, with whom he occasionally worked and lived." —Gordon MacDonald, *Restoring Your Spiritual Passion*

On Your Own and M&M's

Q: The Apostle Paul lived, worked, traveled, and ministered with Priscilla and Aquila. What could they learn from each other (Proverbs 27:17)?

Q: Read Ephesians 4:11–13. Circle the roles of pastors, teachers, and mentors.

Make decisions for you

Encourage unity in faith

Prepare you for works of service — Tell you what to do

Control you — Teach you about God

Build you up — Help you mature spiritually

Q: Read Ecclesiastes 4:9–12 and apply this passage three ways:

- Serving with another person

- Spiritually growing with another person

- Serving and spiritually growing with a spouse

Q: How does associating with other believers stretch you spiritually?

- If you're married, how do you challenge each other to grow spiritually?

Q: Who is the person who has influenced you the most to be the person you are today?

On Your Own

Q: Who keeps you spiritually "sharp" and whom do you sharpen?

M&M's

Q: Have you started serving together in a ministry or doing a project yet? If no, what's stopping you? Pray for God to remove obstacles.

Q: How do you sharpen each other's faith?

Face-to-Face Reflections

Iron sharpening iron is a descriptive definition of mentoring: the concept of using wisdom derived from life experiences, and God, to help each other with whatever life deals us. We all need someone who keeps us on our toes and stretches us. Someone who doesn't let us slack in our walk with God and cares enough to lift us up when we fall, without judging or condemning. Someone whose perspective and insight we value. And the best part: it's a reciprocal relationship!

Personal Parable

A couple's testimony of using what they learned to sharpen other marriages.

Our first ten years of marriage had a worldly focus and foundation for commitment, resulting in trials and challenges to our relationship. After we both accepted Christ, our dream was to serve together working with married couples. We wanted to help them learn from our mistakes and not fall into similar pitfalls. Eventually our dream came true.

We both lack certain qualities, but serving side by side we become whole, and other couples find comfort and hope that if ordinary people like us can make it, so can they. Our imperfections attract most couples, who appreciate our transparency. We communicate how much we rely on keeping God at the center of our marriage relationship, as He uses us to point others to the same place we find our answers—Jesus Christ.

Serving gives us time together, and an opportunity to sharpen each other spiritually as we mature in the Lord together.—Jane and Tom

Mentoring Moment

"Jesus taught that spiritual maturity is never an end in itself. Maturity is for ministry! We grow up in order to give out. It is not enough to keep learning more and more. We must act on what we know and practice what we claim to believe."
— Rick Warren, *The Purpose Driven Life*

Faith in Action

What one thing from this session does God want you to apply in your life today?

Let's Pray Together

Lord, we want humbly to serve You with everything we have—our homes, gifts, jobs, relationships, marriages. Mold us and make us into Your willing servants. We surrender to Your will and Your way. Father, please bring into our life those who will challenge us to grow spiritually and use us to build others up in the faith. Here we are to serve You; here we are to love You. Amen.

SESSION FOUR
FACE-TO-FACE WITH PRISCILLA AND AQUILA: BALANCING LIFE AND MINISTRY

MENTORING TOGETHER

Day One

Discipling

iscipling is a form of mentoring that focuses on helping a new believer grow in biblical knowledge and their relationship with Christ. While Apollos was a scholar, he still had a few things to learn about the Messiah.

Q: How did Priscilla and Aquila "disciple" Apollos (Acts 18:24–26)?

Q: What word picture do these Scriptures use to describe new or regressing Christians?

- 1 Corinthians 3:1–3
- Galatians 4:19–20
- Hebrews 5:12–14
- 1 Peter 2:1–3

Q: Compare an infant's and a new Christian's maturing process. Can either grow without help?

Q: What do disciples of Jesus know (John 8:31–32)?

Q: Did you receive discipling when you were a new Christian? If so, how did that help in your Christian walk? If not, what were the consequences?

On Your Own

Q: How could you find someone to disciple or to disciple you?

M&M's

Q: Would you consider your relationship discipling? Why or why not?

Face-to-Face Reflections

Mentoring can take various forms and focus depending on where the mentee is in his or her Christian life. Discipling of new Christians encompasses making sure they understand the gospel and taking them through a mini course in the Bible so they know where to find answers to their questions. Just as children need parenting, babes in Christ need discipling.

In the *Woman to Woman Mentoring Mentor Handbook,* I reference Bobb Biehl and Glen Urquhart's discussion of the relationship of discipleship to mentoring. In *Mentoring, How to Find a Mentor—How to Become One,* they quote Ted W. Engstrom, coauthor with Norman B. Rohrer, *The Fine Art of Mentoring*:

> 'Discipling' is a close synonym [to mentoring], with these differences: A discipler is one who helps an understudy to

1. give up his own will for the will of God the Father,
2. live daily a life of spiritual sacrifice for the glory of Christ, and
3. strive to be consistently obedient to the commands of his master.

A mentor, on the other hand, provides modeling, close supervision on special projects, individualized help in many areas—discipline, encouragement, correction, confrontation, and a calling to accountability.

Personal Parable

When my daughter Kim and her husband, Toby, were newlyweds and baby Christians, my husband and I discipled them in their newly found faith. We took them through the *Bible for Dummies* and various Navigators' materials. It was a rewarding time that allowed us to help them get off on the right foot in both their marriage and their walk with the Lord.

• • •

Mentoring Moment

"If every mature Christian woman took just one less mature Christian woman for about two years—parenting her, walking alongside her, seeing her do the same for others—exciting things would happen in this church."—A pastor's quote in Lucibel VanAtta's, *Women Encouraging Women: Who Will Disciple Me?*

• • •

Day Two

Instructing and Correcting

The Scriptures admonish us to take action when a fellow Christian compromises his or her faith, feels justified sinning, or needs biblical instruction. God's Word also instructs in how to take action.

On Your Own and M&M's

Q: What does Paul assure us in Romans 15:14?

- How could this verse encourage Priscilla and Aquila to approach Apollos?

Q: How did Priscilla and Aquila use Matthew 18:15 and Paul's approach in Galatians 2:11?

- How effective was Priscilla and Aquila's approach (Acts 18:27–28)?

- Speculate the conversation between the three of them.

Q: Why take action to correct or confront a fellow Christian (2 Timothy 4:1–5)?

- Why do we often hesitate to confront?

- What might have happened to followers of Apollos had he not been corrected?

Q: What are we to use for confronting and instructing (2 Timothy 3:14–17)?

- How will we know the right Scripture for the situation (Psalm 119:11)?

- What tools do most Bibles provide to help find the appropriate Scripture?

Q: If the Holy Spirit is prompting you about someone who needs correcting or instructing, write that person's first name: ____________________.

- What might happen if you don't take action? Can you afford to wait?

Q: Identify corrective approaches in the Personal Parable on the next page and note their effectiveness.

- What methods have worked for you in similar situations?

M&M'S

Q: Mentor, how do you approach corrective or instructive conversations with your mentee?

Q: Mentee, if you don't understand something your mentor says, how can you approach her?

Face-to-Face Reflections

Confronting and instructing are difficult but frequently required in our Christian life, specifically with M&M'S. It's not always the mentee who needs correcting: sometimes a mentor is off base. It's vital that we deal with questionable issues, because like Apollos, mentors are in a position to influence spiritually younger believers.

Before using God's Word to correct and instruct, remember to let the person know you value him or her and the relationship; people don't care how much you know until they know how much you care.

Personal Parable

A friend once asked me what she should do regarding a Christian friend who was living with her boyfriend and seeking a leadership position in a small group. I gave advice from 1 Corinthians 5:1–13 and 2 Timothy 3:14–17 and said, "Many Scriptures call us to accountability in confronting and instructing Christian friends in their sin." The Holy Spirit prompted me to add, "Do it, now!" It was the biblical answer she needed.

I recently read a magazine article about a mom whose son told her that he was moving in with his girlfriend. They were all Christians and the girlfriend had her son attending church again so this development was unexpected. The mom's response was to ask, "May I tell you why I wish you would reconsider?" The son responded, "Yes, I want you to."

Then I came across an advertisement in a magazine where a dad and son are fishing in a boat. The caption above the dad's head says, "Help me understand why some kids your age smoke cigarettes?" The caption below the picture says, "There are many ways to start a conversation with your kids about not smoking. But the important thing is to get the conversation going. So talk to them today about staying away from cigarettes. How to start the conversation is up to you."

• • •

Mentoring Moment

Asking questions is an effective way to start a corrective conversation. The answering process often allows the other person an opportunity to arrive at a satisfactory conclusion, which becomes his or her own idea.

• • •

Day Three

Being Sensitive and Receptive

Spiritual maturity evolves from humbly admitting we don't know everything and willingly soaking in all we can learn from those who have gone before us.

On Your Own and M&M's

Q: In Acts 18:26, how do Priscilla and Aquila show sensitivity (Ephesians 4:15)?

- What was the significance of taking Apollos home?

- How important is timing in approaching someone (Ecclesiastes 3:1, 7*b*)?

Q: Paul sends Timothy to reprimand the church in 1 Corinthians 4:17–21. What choices did Paul give them regarding his visit (v. 21)?

- What does Paul warn about some of their attitudes (v. 18)?

- What does their attitude make them (Proverbs 18:2)?

- What could happen to the church (Proverbs 11:2–3; 16:18)?

Q: Apollos was a renowned and eloquent teacher (Acts 18:24–25). Priscilla and Aquila were tentmakers. What can we presume about Apollos from his receptiveness to their wise counsel?

- Proverbs 9:9–10

- Proverbs 10:17

- Proverbs 15:31–32

- Proverbs 19:8, 20, 25, 27

Q: How do we know Apollos listened and learned (Acts 18:27–28; 1 Corinthians 3:4–6, 22; 4:6; 16:12)?

- How effective would his teaching have been if he hadn't been receptive (Proverbs 5:12–14; 15:22)?

- How are both the giver and receiver of correction rewarded (Proverbs 25:12)?

Q: Read the Personal Parable on page 84. What are similarities in the way Priscilla and Aquila corrected Apollos and Beth corrected me?

- What feelings do you think Priscilla, Aquila, and Beth had to overcome?
- What risks did they take?
- Why do you think they took action anyway?

Q: Note what these verses advise regarding receptiveness.

- Proverbs 1:5, 7
- Proverbs 23:12
- 1 Thessalonians 5:12–13

Q: Does the message change if the person is not receptive? Explain.

Q: Describe when someone wasn't sensitive in correcting you. How did you feel?

- How did you receive the counsel?

Q: What have you learned about giving and receiving instruction or correction?

M&M'S

Q: Mentor, your sensitivity influences your mentee's receptiveness. How can you discern the right time and place for discussing an issue?

Q: Mentee, being a learner requires humility and a receptive heart. Help your mentor know when you're ready to discuss a sensitive subject, but don't put it off too long.

Face-to-Face Reflections

Apollos was a gifted, talented, zealous young teacher and orator, who would preach to many people in the future. Priscilla and Aquila knew it was vital that he have the complete message. The Holy Spirit opened their ears to hear the error in his teaching and gave them the courage and tactfulness to approach and lovingly correct him privately. The Holy Spirit gave Apollos the ears and heart to hear.

Occasionally, a mentor laments, "I don't know how I can help my mentee: she's successful, smart, and seems to have it all together." Success and intelligence don't make a mature Christian. Mentoring is a two-way relationship; however, it can never take place without the mentee's willing receptiveness to the wisdom of the mentor. If a mentee becomes defensive and refuses to take suggestions or advice, or the mentor is insensitive or haughty, it thwarts the relationship.

A mentor isn't responsible for her mentee's choices or actions, but she is responsible for presenting the Lord's perspective in the Lord's way.

Personal Parable

During a Woman to Woman Mentoring training in Tennessee, one of our former Saddleback M&M'S who had moved to the area attended the conference. During the training, Beth heard me give the wrong Scripture reference for a passage. After the conference, Beth accompanied my cotrainer and me at dinner. As we chatted, she mentioned recently studying the passage I referred to and gently said she thought I gave the wrong reference.

"Really? I don't think so, Beth, but I'll check on it," I said, still thinking I was right. She didn't make an issue of it, but still maintained she was sure she was correct.

When I returned home, the Holy Spirit reminded me to double-check that passage, and Beth was right. I had quoted it wrong! Beth respects me as a leader and a teacher, and I have been a Christian much longer than her, and yet, she was willing to lovingly correct me—not to show she was smarter than me, but to prevent me from making the same error again.

I thanked Beth for bravely and boldly confronting me. Like Apollos, I wouldn't want to continue giving incomplete or inaccurate information.

• • •

Mentoring Moment

Whenever we think we've learned it all,
we're headed for a big fall.

• • •

Day Four

Couples Mentoring

"Our marriage has been strengthened and enriched, because mentoring others keeps us 'on our toes.' We cannot walk in integrity before others if we aren't committed to growth in our marriage. No, we don't have to be perfect or have it all together; but we believe we can make a difference by living out God's plan for our marriage—to grow more into being one."—Jan and Gene Ebel

On Your Own and M&M's

Q: How does Genesis 2:24 echo the above statement of Jan and Gene Ebel?

- How did Priscilla and Aquila reflect this verse?

Q: What symbolism does the Bible use for marriage (Isaiah 61:10; 62:5; Revelation 19:6–9; 21:1–3)?

- Why is it important for Christian marriages to be a good witness?

- If you're single, who is your Bridegroom (Isaiah 54:5)?

Q: Read Titus 2:1–8. How does this passage support couples mentoring couples?

- What topics should they discuss?

- How might this lead to godly marriages (Titus 2:11 to 3:2)?

- How could rifts in marriages be healed (Titus 3:3–8)?

- List benefits of engaged couples receiving mentoring from married couples.

Q: How did Priscilla and Aquila live out Titus 3:13–14?

- Note, their former mentee evidently brought Paul's letter to Titus (Titus 3:13).

On Your Own

Q: If you're married or dating, have you participated in couples mentoring as the mentors or mentees? If so, how did you benefit?

- If not, speculate potential blessings to the mentor and mentee couples.

M&M'S

Q: If you're both married or dating, consider meeting as couples to discuss marriage or dating issues. What are benefits and/or drawbacks?

Face-to-Face Reflections

Mentoring as a couple requires a strong Christ-centered marriage in which *both* spouses have a good relationship with the Lord, and each other. Then, if they're willing, God uses their life experiences as preparation for mentoring other couples. Jan and Gene Ebel share ways couples mentoring relationships can develop:

- We first started mentoring by informally counseling newly married couples, or couples hitting rough spots, who gravitated toward us.
- We had a solid foundation for our marriage and loving Christian parents who were our role models.
- Our marriage wasn't perfect, but we were committed to working together to make it better.
- Our transparency and honesty about our own struggles made couples feel safe with us.
- We usually mentor one couple at a time, but when we taught marriage principles in our church, the openness and interaction in the class actually became a mentoring experience.
- Couples in small groups we've participated in have mentored each other.
- A mentoring relationship can develop from a couple being in crisis. We initially do some lay counseling, and then continue meeting for dinner or coffee to follow up.

Personal Parable

In this excerpt from "Ordinary Couples, Extraordinary Influence" in *The First Five Years,* Bill and Pam Farrel discuss the mentoring they received from a couple whose marriage was a witness to these newlyweds.

> They [Tom and Barbara Buck] were engaged in a real relationship with Pam and me. Pam saw another wonderful model, like her mother, of a woman who lived out Proverbs 31 in her love for God and her willingness to work hard. I saw in Tom an example of a man who was kind, productive, godly, and courageous. He supported Barbara in her pursuits but was willing to put his foot down when necessary. Barbara was also willing to encourage us when we did what was right and confront us in areas we needed to grow.
>
> For me (Pam), I needed to see in action a man my father's age who was truly kind, caring and calm. Watching how Tom gently served and encouraged Barbara gave me hope that I too could have a marriage that was the "happily ever after" kind. Tom's daily expressions of love toward Barbara, and his affirmations to me in a daughter-like way bolstered my confidence that Bill and I could have the kind of long-lasting love they shared.

• • •

Mentoring Moment

Marriage is a reflection of Jesus Christ and His church—Christ is the head of your home.

• • •

Day Five

God Working Through You

"In an age when the focus is mostly on what happens *between* husband and wife, Aquila and Priscilla are an example of what can happen *through* a husband and wife."
—*Life Application Study Bible, New Living Translation*

On Your Own and M&M's

Q: What are rewards of investing in others' spiritual growth?

- Proverbs 12:14
- Jeremiah 17:10
- 1 Corinthians 3:8
- Colossians 3:23–24
- 1 Peter 5:2–4

Q: What rewards do you think Priscilla and Aquila received (Acts 18:27–28; Romans 16:3–4)?

Q: Apply 1 Corinthians 3:6–9*a* to mentoring:

- Who planted the seed of faith in your life?

- Who is watering that seed?

- How is God growing the seed?

Q: What are we to do when God helps us through difficult times (2 Corinthians 1:3–5)?

- Describe a time you received comfort from someone with a similar experience.

- When has God used your experiences to share His comfort with others?

- What "reward" did you receive?

On Your Own

Q: Identify an area in your life or marriage where God could work through your experiences to help someone else.

M&M's

Q: Mentor, has someone planted the seed of faith in your mentee's life, or is that your calling?

- How will *you* water the seed and let God grow it?

- If you're not seeing growth, what might be missing?

- Whose responsibility is it to make things happen in her life? Explain.

- What steps can you take to ensure you never overstep God in your mentee's life?

- What "rewards" have you experienced as a mentor?

Q: Mentee, explain how 1 Corinthians 3:6–9*a* applies personally to you and your mentor.

- How does it feel knowing your mentor can't make changes in your life—only God and you can?

Face-to-Face Reflections

After Priscilla and Aquila led Apollos to a deeper knowledge of Christ, he returned to the Synagogue and corrected his original message. His listeners didn't chastise him, but instead recognized his spiritual growth and recommended him to go speak to other churches. Perhaps Priscilla and Aquila even helped write the letter of recommendation. Apollos left the believers at Ephesus, and moved on to debate with the unbelieving Jews in Achaia. Armed with the full story, he convinced many of them that Jesus was the risen Messiah.

It didn't take much discipling before Apollos was back on the road again preaching, teaching, and saving lives. Paul commended Priscilla and Aquila: *"all the churches of the Gentiles are grateful to them."* What rewarding, fulfilling joy this must have been to Priscilla and Aquila!

I've had the opportunity to disciple many new believers, and it's thrilling to run into them later and see how God has grown them. My husband and I testify that you can't put a dollar value on the lives we've seen changed and enhanced through mentoring.

Personal Parable

Excerpts from "Just a Few Years Older and Wiser" in Bill and Pam Farrel's *The First Five Years*.

> Bill and Tina Wilcox...were serving in a campus ministry in central California when I (Pam) was attending junior college. Tina took a personal interest in me. She taught me the basic spiritual disciplines: how to have a quiet time with God, how to pray, how to share my faith with others, and how to walk in the power of the Holy Spirit.
>
> Their impact was especially important as Bill and I started dating. Because Bill and I grew up in dysfunctional homes, we were aware that we really didn't know how to have healthy relationships. To head off the influence of our families, we both had to learn to be very deliberate in our decision making when it came to our relationship. Bill and Tina met with us and encouraged us to ask the hard questions of each other, to pursue books,

people and resources to heal the holes in each of our hearts. Bill and Tina held us accountable to take those steps of growth, often checking up on our progress.

In many ways, we are who we are today because of this "ordinary" couple.

Mentoring Moment

"The satisfaction of knowing we are fulfilling God's purpose for our marriage through mentoring is so rich. Knowing that marriages have actually been saved and children have been spared the pain of divorce perhaps because of our taking the time with these couples is something for which we will forever thank the Lord."

—Jan and Gene Ebel

Let's Pray Together

Dear Father, You tell us in Your Word that one generation is to teach and train the next. We want to honor that command by allowing You to use us to disciple and mentor others. Provide us with opportunities to share with others how You have walked beside us through life's circumstances and You want to walk beside them also. Bring into our lives those who need a stronger faith, and challenge us to learn from others who have gone before us. Amen.

SESSION FIVE
FACE-TO-FACE WITH PRISCILLA AND AQUILA: BALANCING LIFE AND MINISTRY

BALANCING LIFE AND MINISTRY

Day One

Teamwork

Priscilla and Aquila were a team in marriage, work, and ministry; and Paul was on their business team.

On Your Own and M&M's

Q: What is the significance of Priscilla's and Aquila's names always mentioned together?

Q: List names that always go together today—don't limit this to married couples.

- What, if anything, did each "team" accomplish together?

Q: Read 1 Corinthians 12:4–6, 14–22. List benefits of working as a team versus on your own.

- Explain the equality of team members (1 Corinthians 12:25–26).

Q: How does marriage require teamwork?

Q: Why did Jesus send the disciples out in pairs (Mark 6:7)?

Q: What did the following biblical teams accomplish for the Lord?

Team	Accomplishments
Moses and Aaron (Exodus 4:14–15; 7:1–7; 12:50–51; 17:8–13)	
Deborah and Barak (Judges 4:4–16)	
Naomi and Ruth (Ruth 1:16–19; 3:1–6; 4:13–18)	
Esther and Mordecai (Esther 2:7–11, 15–17; 3:5–6; 4:1–8; 8:3–8)	
Mary and Joseph (Matthew 1:18–24)	
Paul and Barnabas (Acts 11:25–26)	

Q: When has working as a team, or being part of a team, helped you balance life and ministry?

M&M'S

Q: Do you feel like a team? Why or why not?

Q: Mentor, how can you assure your mentee never feels inferior to you?

Q: Mentee, lovingly inform your mentor if you feel she is condescending.

Face-to-Face Reflections

You probably noted that teamwork helps balance life and ministry because teams can be: efficient, supportive, united, all-inclusive in skills, or work requires more than one person. Sue and Larry Richards in their book, *Every Woman in the Bible*, discuss the marital teamwork of Priscilla and Aquila and how it relates to their ministering together:

> As a Jewish wife, Priscilla would have been expected to be subject to her husband. Aquila would have been the one who studied God's Law and who sat with the other men in the synagogue. Priscilla would have been expected to know the laws governing a kosher kitchen, but in all the other matters, she would have been expected to defer to her husband. In mentioning the couple, if both were mentioned at all, normal mode of speech would have identified Aquila "and his wife." But here in the New Testament not only is Priscilla identified by name, she is frequently mentioned first.
>
> The easy exchange of the names of Priscilla and Aquila makes it clear that Priscilla was a full partner with her husband in ministry. She did not dominate him, but neither did he dominate her. Aquila and Priscilla's marriage as portrayed here adds insight to the changed status of women in Christianity. Without "lowering" the man, the new faith exalted the woman, making them partners in ministry as well as in life.

Likewise, in M&M teams, even though the mentor takes spiritual leadership and responsibility for the relationship, the mentor isn't superior to the mentee. The mentor is simply further along her journey with the Lord and can impart wisdom learned along the way.

Personal Parable

A story of a couple who, like Priscilla and Aquila, are a team in marriage, work, and ministry.

Initially working together created a series of struggles: Debbie liked structure and I (Jerry) preferred independence. I had difficulty turning projects over to her and not interfering with how she performed the job. Our different styles created daily conflict in which Debbie resigned, or I fired her, several times a week. We laugh now, but it wasn't funny then.

We eventually overcame the challenges and learned how to work as a team and not two individuals. We recognized that our work in real estate was a ministry in which God could use us in helping people with a major life decision.

When the opportunity arose to serve together in a premarital counseling ministry, we knew God wanted to use our life experience of broken marriages to help others build their marriage upon our Rock, Jesus Christ. We had been working successfully together in real estate for several years by then and transitioned easily to counseling couples together, which reciprocally ministers to our marriage. Being used by God as a team to mentor other couples brings us tremendous joy as we prepare them for the second most important commitment of their lives: the first, being their commitment to Jesus.

Mentoring Moment

"Couples who are united in Christ can have a great impact together for His kingdom. God can work mightily through a couple who are devoted to Christ and willing to use their time, efforts, and resources to build God's kingdom."
—Tim Clinton, *The Soul Care Bible*

Day Two

Taking Your Faith to Work

It's probable that Priscilla, Aquila, and Paul didn't separate their professional and ministry life. Perhaps that's why medical doctor Luke, the author of Acts and contemporary of Paul, included details about their careers as role models of taking faith to work and working their faith.

On Your Own and M&M's

Q: What evidence is there that God works (Genesis 2:2–3; Psalm 104:1–32)?

Q: How are we to promote God's work (Psalm 145:4–6)?

- How could this command be incorporated into work life (Proverbs 31:16–18)?

- Into keeping house and raising kids (Proverbs 31:11–14, 31)?

Q: Who created "work" (Genesis 3:23; Psalm 104:23)?

- What value does God put on work (Proverbs 22:29)?

Q: How did Paul model that work and ministry are not exclusive (2 Thessalonians 3:6–10)?

Q: How do these verses put in perspective the world's work and God's work?

- Romans 16:12–13

- 1 Corinthians 15:58

Q: Note how Paul's teachings synchronize the Lord's work with career work.

	PRISCILLA AND AQUILA	YOU (AT HOME/JOB)
2 Corinthians 9:8		
Colossians 3:23		
1 Thessalonians 1:3		
1 Thessalonians 4:11		

Q: Proverbs 16:10–12 (*The Message*) encourages: *"A good leader motivates, doesn't mislead, doesn't exploit. GOD cares about honesty in the workplace; your business is his business. Good leaders abhor wrongdoing of all kinds; sound leadership has a moral foundation."* Underline the phrases that display a godly worker/leader.

- Do you have concerns about taking your faith to work—whether in the home or workplace? Why or why not?

- List practical ways of witnessing at work by following God's principles.

M&M's

Q: Discuss struggles either of you have with being a woman of faith at work or at home. How could you help each other?

Face-to-Face Reflections

God created work: it isn't the result of Adam and Eve's sin. The couple tended to God's garden before they ate the forbidden fruit—work just became harder after their fall from grace. God wants us to be productive, provide for ourselves, enjoy the fruits of our labor, and be a good witness whether it's at home with children, in the office with co-workers, or anywhere He plants us.

Today's laws often prohibit sharing our faith at work, but there is no law against letting your faith shine through your attitude, work ethic, honesty, humbleness, communication, kindness, and by not participating in gossip or slander. If you work, in the home or out of the home, as if you were working directly for the Lord, people will notice and want to know more about what motivates you: a perfect opportunity to invite them to your house for dinner or out to lunch and let them know the real CEO of your life.

In His sovereignty, God has placed you into the culture He wants to infiltrate. Don't let work interfere with your witness; let how you work be your witness.

Personal Profile

In her book, *Women, Faith, and Work*, Lois Flowers shares the story of Hollywood producer, Karen Covell.

> As Karen grew in her faith and began her career, she became increasingly convinced that God *had* called her to be a missionary. But she wasn't called

to the jungles of Africa. She was called to work in another mission field—the entertainment industry.

Eighteen years ago, she and her husband helped found a prayer group whose members meet once a month to pray for the industry, their work, and their colleagues. Now called PREMISE, this group's meetings attract seventy to eighty people. And for the last decade, the couple has been teaching a lifestyle evangelism class in their home that is geared specifically to entertainment industry professionals.

The Covells also speak frequently to college audiences, churches, and professional groups around the country, encouraging people of faith to view the entertainment business as a mission field.

• • •

Mentoring Moment

"A dairy maid can milk cows to the glory of God."
—Martin Luther

"It's not what a man does that determines
whether his work is sacred or secular,
it is why he does it."
—A. W. Tozer

• • •

Day Three

Balancing or Juggling?

alancing can be as precarious as juggling: it takes so little to upset balance and eventually jugglers drop the ball.

On Your Own and M&M's

Q: Read Matthew 11:29–30. What does Jesus teach about balanced living?

Q: Paul worked with Priscilla and Aquila during the week, but what did he do *every* Sabbath (Acts 18:4)?

Q: Even God fit a day of rest into His work week, and He asked us to do the same (Exodus 20:9–11; Hebrews 4:9–11)—do you? Why or why not?

- What are we to do while we rest from work on the Sabbath, and what is the blessing (Isaiah 58:13–14)?

- Explain why any day we set aside to rest and refuel mentally, physically, and spiritually is our Sabbath (Mark 2:27).

Q: Read Matthew 5:37. What does this verse imply regarding obligations?

- What determines your yes or no to a new request or opportunity (Philippians 4:6)?

- When might no be the right answer to good, fun, or even ministry opportunities?

- Sometimes delegating is the right answer. In Acts 6:1–7, describe how the 12 disciples delegated and the result.

Q: When you became a Christian, what did you "put off" from your old self (Ephesians 4:22–24)?

- Describe the "new self" you put on.

- What happens if you don't replace one way of living with another?

- How could taking a Sabbath, saying no occasionally, and delegating make room for new ways of living?

Q: How often did the first church meet (Acts 2:46; 5:42)?

- What could you "put off" to have a daily quiet time with the Lord?

Q: What happens when balanced scales have something added to one side without removing anything from the other side?

- What obligations and activities have you added instead of replacing?

- Describe your attitude when juggling activities and relationships.

- How could God's ways restore "balance" in your life?

Q: Mark on your calendar: daily quiet times, weekly church attendance, small-group meetings, and a "Sabbath" day off. What needs to be removed to make time for these spiritual disciplines?

M&M's

Q: Talk about areas where your life is out of balance. Mentor, provide tips and suggestions. Make notes.

Q: You added M&M meetings to your calendar: what did you take off?

Face-to-Face Reflections

When I told my husband about my desire to attend seminary, he pointed out that we still had children at home and I had a full-time career. He wisely asked me what I was willing to give up in my schedule to make room for seminary. Likewise, when women want to be in an M&M relationship, we counsel that mentoring isn't something you fit into an already overcrowded calendar. Mentoring is a commitment, and we want M&M'S to pray about what they'll give up to add this new blessing to their life.

The concept of balance in our life is a struggle for most of us. In a *Parade Magazine* article by Jeanne Wolf, "Jennifer Garner: 'I Need to Find Balance,'" Garner, a married actress and mother of two young children was lamenting that the job she loves sometimes causes her to miss bedtimes. "My sisters both are working mothers," she says. "I understand that my being an actress as well as being at home isn't some heroic thing. That doesn't mean it isn't confusing or difficult—especially that question of how you find a balance."

God created balance and He didn't mean for it to be elusive. The Bible is an instruction manual on balanced living: spending time in it, and with its Author, is the answer to achieving balance and eliminating juggling.

Personal Parable

Jan and Gene Ebel's story continued:

> Before children, we both worked full-time and did ministry on off hours. We might be tired after work and not want to meet with a couple, but we honored our commitments and did "the right thing." When we were faithful to what God asked of us, He always provided the energy. But when our children were young, we didn't balance ministry and family—didn't say no when we should have. We tried to do too much.
>
> We learned that God doesn't call you to minister to *every* couple that comes along. It's important to pray before making a commitment: asking

the Lord if He has sent this couple. Occasionally couples in crisis would call while we were at work, and we followed the scriptural admonition to "work as unto the Lord" and set boundaries. We would quickly pray with the person and make an appointment to contact them later. Setting boundaries was mentoring: a role model of balancing work and ministry.

Mentoring Moment

"The season of life you are in right now
should guide your decisions about where to spend your time."
—Brenda Lancaster, *Living in a Zoo?*

Day Four

Prioritizing

"Busyness is a great enemy of relationships. We become preoccupied with making a living, doing our work, paying bills, and accomplishing goals as if these tasks are the point of life. They are not. The point of life is learning to love—God and people."
—Rick Warren, *The Purpose Driven Life*

On Your Own and M&M's

Q: How does God say to prioritize life (Matthew 22:36–39)?

Q: Read Isaiah 40:11–12. How important is God's work (v. 12)?

- What does He still make time for (v. 11)?

- What is the significance of relationships listed *before* accomplishments?

Q: What could Priscilla and Aquila learn from how Paul prioritized his life (Acts 18:3–4, 7–8; 2 Corinthians 12:14–15)?

Q: What do these verses instruct about prioritizing?

- Isaiah 55:2

- Matthew 6:21

- Matthew 16:25–27

Q: Place these 12 items in order of their value to you by marking an X under a number—1 = high and 12 = low. (There can only be one X under each number)

	1	2	3	4	5	6	7	8	9	10	11	12
God's Word												
Generosity												
Money												
Family												
Serving												
Witnessing												
House												
Appearance												
Friends												
Career												
Possessions												
Ministry												

- Using the 1–12 scale, mark *P&A* under the numbers, in the order you think Priscilla and Aquila most valued these items.

- Consider your calendar of activities. Using the 1–12 rating scale, and the items on this list, write a *T* next to the activities where you spend time.

- Look at your checkbook: under the 1–12 rating scale, put a *$* by where you spend the least to the most money.

- What changes can you make to align your values with your time and expenditures?

Q: How will you reprioritize to focus on relationships and serving, while honoring family and work?

M&M's

Q: Review the value rating exercise and discuss how to keep each other accountable in making necessary changes.

Face-to-Face Reflections

We all have the same number of hours each day, but we don't all have the same number of hours in a lifetime. Every day, every minute, we make choices as to how we will spend our gift of a moment—and when it's gone, we can never get it back. It's sobering to look at our day and see the wasted time.

Being a Christian requires a commitment to spiritual growth, service, and sharing the good news. In her monthly Renewal Ministries newsletter, Anne Ortlund shares a practical example of prioritizing from one of her mentees: "Thank you [Anne] for challenging me to change my priority yesterday. Had I kept my [original] goal I would have rushed off to the gym this morning and missed the much-needed unhurried time I spent in the Word and in prayer. I will take a walk this evening with my wonderful husband."

Personal Parable

Jan and Gene Ebel caution young couples that family must be priority. "Our daughter and son-in-law do well in this area by working their ministry to younger couples into their friendships and social times. They invite families to beach outings, potlucks at their home, etc. and share together as the children play."

A couple in a small group Dave and I were leading asked their children if they wanted Daddy to work overtime so they could have money to build a pool in the backyard. In unison the kids yelled, "No!" They would rather have Daddy home with them than a swimming pool. Those children had their priorities right.

Mentoring Moment

The things that count most in life
are the things that cannot be counted. —Anonymous

Day Five

A Way of Life

Priscilla and Aquila availed themselves and their home for mentoring and teaching the gospel everywhere they went. Ministry was a way of life.

On Your Own and M&M's

Q: Whose lives did Priscilla and Aquila touch (Romans 16:4*b*)?

Q: Read 1 Thessalonians 2:4–9, 11–13. Who is pleased when we share the gospel with others (v. 4)?

- What should be our motivation to help others (v. 6)?

- How does a "mother caring for her children" portray mentoring (v. 7)?

Q: How did Priscilla and Aquila live out Matthew 6:2?

Q: Read Mark 14:3–9. Focusing on verse 8, *"she did what she could,"* how does this story encourage you to use what you have for the Lord?

Q: What is the common theme of these verses?

- 1 Corinthians 4:16–17

- 1 Corinthians 11:1

- Hebrews 13:7

Q: Explain how living a life worth imitating (*imitable life*) is a ministry.

Q: Read Galatians 5:22–23. What's the observable fruit of a Christian's way of life?

- How does your "way of life" influence others?

- How does your "way of life" glorify God?

Q: Describe how pleasing God will balance your life and ministry.

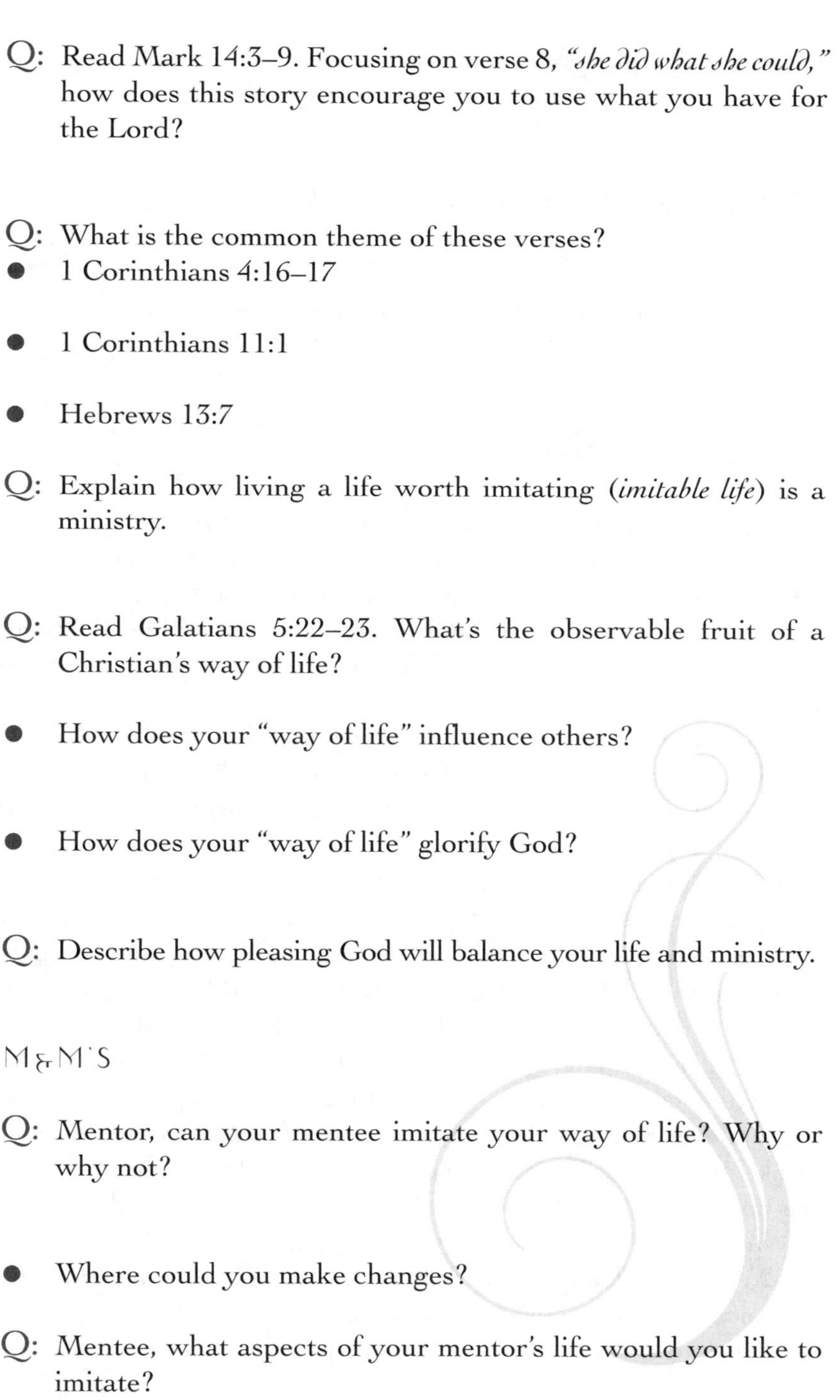

M&M'S

Q: Mentor, can your mentee imitate your way of life? Why or why not?

- Where could you make changes?

Q: Mentee, what aspects of your mentor's life would you like to imitate?

Q: Mentor, when your mentee is ready to mentor others, why is your "work" not finished?

- How can you encourage your mentee to become a mentor?

Q: Mentee, how will you pass on what you've learned from your mentor?

Face-to-Face Reflections

A way of life that glorifies God and helps lead others to Him is the "secret" to balancing life and ministry. You don't need to serve on a committee or church staff to be a witness for Christ in your neighborhood, workplace, family, home... wherever life takes you. God's character shines through His works: He expects the same of us.

But God doesn't want us working for Him until we have a relationship with Him, and that relationship should *enhance,* not *encroach on,* all our earthly relationships. That means being a loving parent, spouse, worker, neighbor, friend, M&M, Bible study group member, daughter—every aspect of life should reflect Jesus.

Then you're ready to step out of your comfort zone, and let God use you to plant seeds, water, and cultivate—like Priscilla and Aquila, Paul, Apollos, Dave and me, and the couples who shared with you in this study—and God will do the harvesting. He'll make His Spirit grow fruit in lives that your way of life influences. Look around you, there are struggling men and women everywhere: *"The harvest is plentiful, but the workers are few"* (Luke 10:2). Maybe you're one of those couples needing mentoring and wise counsel. Find godly marriages that you admire and ask one of those couples if they would spend time with you.

My husband and I strive to have our way of life be a mentoring role model of a Christian marriage for our four children and their spouses and everyone *God* puts in our path. I challenge you to do likewise.

Personal Parable

A Woman to Woman Mentoring M&M testimony of a couple's "way of life" impacting a mentee's unbelieving husband.

I felt I couldn't mentor because my husband's job was uncertain and we might have to move. But God nudged me to make myself available and trust Him to take care of everything.

I was matched with a new Christian with an unbelieving husband. Our children were the same age, allowing us to meet with the kids and attend church together. Then biweekly, not to inconvenience her husband, we met for a Bible study. My mentee had wisdom on when to speak and when to remain quiet with her husband—something she taught me. My husband needed me to stop trying to fix things and allow him to talk about his problems and worries.

A mentor should be open and honest with her mentee so I shared that when I wanted to shout "Why?" at God, I had learned to stop and praise Him instead. I told our small group that if my mentee's husband came to know the Lord by my husband and my witness, then our struggles were worth it. Not long after this, her husband started coming to church with us. I can still remember when he decided to trust Jesus with his life and how tears of joy ran down our faces.

We have shared with this precious couple that even when you're obeying God, not everything goes as you want—but with God, we can get through everything and grow along the way. Being a mentor has kept me focused on God and looking for how He wants me to mature as a wife and in my faith.

Mentoring Moment

"It is not your business to succeed, but to do right;
when you have done so,
the rest lies with God."—C. S. Lewis

Mentoring is simply living an imitable life
that points others to God.

Let's Pray Together

Personalize and pray Colossians 1:9–12:
"For this reason, since the day we heard about you, we have not stopped praying for you and asking God to fill you with the knowledge of his will through all spiritual wisdom and understanding. And we pray this in order that you may live a life worthy of the Lord and may please him in every way: bearing fruit in every good work, growing in the knowledge of God, being strengthened with all power according to his glorious might so that you may have great endurance and patience, and joyfully giving thanks to the Father, who has qualified you to share in the inheritance of the saints in the kingdom of light." Amen.

A Twenty-First-Century Priscilla and Aquila Testimony

One night my husband, Frank, was on a business trip when our couples' small-group Bible study met, leaving me (Amy) to lead the group. I was simultaneously anxious and excited. During our group discussion, a husband drifted off the subject. His wife kindly tried to steer him back on topic, but he told her to shut up. The rest of the evening was tense and quiet.

When Frank called after group, I shared what happened. He replied, "We need to address this right away, one-on-one with the couple."

The night arrived when the four of us sat face-to-face in our living room. Frank prayed a simple prayer of thanksgiving for this couple in our lives and for Jesus to join our discussion. First, we affirmed our love for them as valuable group members, and then I explained the small-group incident we wanted to explore.

After several attempts from the husband to minimize the issue, get Frank to side with him, and declare he wasn't going to change for anyone, he finally relinquished, "I guess we're in this group to learn more about how to communicate with one another."

The couple continued in our small group and the husband kept his stories short and to the point and honored his wife and others in the group.

CLOSING MATERIALS

Doing Life Together

We Conclude Our Study of Priscilla and Aquila

Let's Pray a Closing Prayer Together

Dear Lord, You are the Master Mentor. Help us always look to You for direction, guidance, and wisdom. Lord we want to reflect Your love and kindness to others. Help us to be the kind of person or couple that others respect and to take the risk of confronting a Christian sister or brother who needs correction. Give us the warmth and openness to share with others our life, heart, home, and You, God. In our marriages, help us work as a team and remain united in action and in spirit with You at the center of our relationship and our life.

Father, please guide us as we seek Your will for the next step after this study. How are we to use what we have learned? Where would You have us serve? We want to mentor and be mentored in the way You show us in the Bible. We know that with Your encouragement and direction anything is possible. Amen.

Janet's Suggestions

Congratulations! You are well on your way to balancing life and ministry. If you've completed the study "On Your Own," hopefully you feel equipped to be a mentor, or maybe find a mentor for yourself. If you're married, God could be calling you to start a couples mentoring relationship.

Also, consider that maybe you're ready to take a group through this study as the facilitator and leader by utilizing the Leader's Guide starting on pages 122. Whatever you do, don't put this study away and forget about it. God had a purpose in leading you to the story of Priscilla and Aquila. Go back through the book and put on your calendar any commitments you made and make plans to apply points that were especially pertinent to you.

If you're married, remember that your marriage is a witness and role model to everyone you meet. Always be aware that others are watching to see what a Christian marriage looks like. Remain alert and open to ways you can serve in ministry together, as well as on your own.

Use the Prayer & Praise Journal at the end of the book. Record your spiritual journey and what you have seen the Lord do in your life. For M&M'S, this will be a legacy of your mentoring relationship.

For further reading:

- *Women, Faith, and Work: How Ten Successful Professionals Blend Belief and Business* by Lois Flowers (Word Publishing, 2001).
- *Praying for Your Prodigal Daughter: Hope, Help, and Encouragement for Hurting Parents* by Janet Thompson (Howard Books/Simon & Schuster, 2008). Read the miraculous story of praying home my prodigal daughter Kim. I also offer encouragement and tips to help parents of prodigals pray for their daughters.
- *Dear God, They Say It's Cancer: A Companion Guide for Women on the Breast Cancer Journey* by Janet Thompson (Howard Books/Simon & Schuster, 2006). My opportunity to mentor other breast cancer sisters from my own journey.
- *Woman to Woman Mentoring How to Start, Grow, and Maintain a Mentoring Ministry DVD Leader Kit* is available at your local LifeWay bookstore or at www.lifeway.com or by calling 1-800-458-2772.

Additional "Face-to-Face" Bible Studies:

- *Face-to-Face with Mary and Martha: Sisters in Christ*
- *Face-to-Face with Naomi and Ruth: Together for the Journey*
- *Face-to-Face with Elizabeth and Mary: Generation to Generation*
- *Face-to-Face with Euodia and Syntyche: From Conflict to Community*

To learn more about AHW Ministries, Janet's writing and speaking ministry, visit www.womantowomanmentoring.com.

Leader's Guide

for Group-Study Facilitators and M&M's

Suggestions for Facilitators

Congratulations! God has appointed you the awesome privilege of setting the pace and focus for this group. Regardless of how many groups you have facilitated, this group will be a new and unique experience. This guide's suggestions and tips have helped me, and I trust they also will benefit you. Change or adapt them as you wish, but they are a solid place to start.

Organizing the Sessions

Small groups generally meet in a home, and larger churchwide groups usually meet at the church or other facility. I suggest for the larger group that you form small groups by sitting everyone at round tables. Appoint or ask for a volunteer facilitator for each table and have the group sit together for the five sessions of this study. Then both small-group leaders and large-group table facilitators can use the following format.

1. **Starting the sessions**—In my experience, members usually come in rushed, harried, and someone is always late—creating the perplexing dilemma of when to start. I suggest beginning on time because you are committed to ending on time. Don't wait for the last late person to arrive. Waiting dishonors those who arrive on time and sets the precedent that it's OK to be a little late because "they won't start without me, anyway." Also, if you delay the start time, you may not finish the discussion.

2. **Icebreakers**—Each session has an "icebreaker" that is fun, interactive, helps the group become acquainted, and encourages on-time arrivals. It's an interactive activity participants won't want to miss. The icebreaker also eases group members out of their hectic day and into a study mode.
3. **Format**—Each session includes: Opening Prayer, Icebreaker, Five Days of Selected Discussion Questions, Prayer, Fellowship.
4. **The Session Guide provides you with:**

- Preparation: what you need to do or obtain in advance.
- Icebreakers: openers for each meeting.
- Bold: the action you need to say or take.
- Ideas: to help facilitate discussion and suggest answers that might be less obvious.
- Session name, day, and page number: to identify area discussed.

5. **Suggested time**—Each session has nine numbered activities. Fifteen minutes on each number equals a two-hour meeting. This is a guideline to modify according to your time allotment. Let the Holy Spirit guide you and cover what seems applicable and pertinent to your group.
6. **Facilitating discussion**—Questions and Scriptures to discuss are only a suggestion to enhance what participants have studied on their own already. Feel free to cover whatever material you think or the group feels is pertinent. Think about ways to:

- Keep all engaged in conversation.
- Avoid "rabbit trails."
- Assure each one has a clear understanding of the points under discussion.
- Encourage members to stay accountable by doing their lesson and arriving on time.

Big job you say! You can do it with God's help and strength.

7. **Prayertime**—Prayer should be an ongoing and vital part of your group. Open and close your times together in prayer. There is a prayer at the end of each session to pray together. Taking prayer requests can often get lengthy and be a source of gossip, if not handled properly. Let me share with you a way that works well in groups:

- At the end of the meeting, give each woman an index card and instruct her to write *one* prayer request pertaining to the study and pass the card to the leader/facilitator. Mix up the cards and have each person pick one. If someone picks her own card, have her put it back in the pile and pick a different one.

- When everyone has a card, go around the group (or table) and each person is to read the name and prayer request on her card so others can write down the requests. Participants may want to use the Prayer & Praise Journal starting on page 138.
- Instruct the group to hold hands and agree in unison as each participant prays the prayer request for the person whose card she has. This allows everyone to experience praying.
- Each woman takes home the card she received and prays for that person, ongoing.
- As the leader/facilitator, pray between meetings for the group, your leadership, and ask God to mentor you and the members. And have fun!

8. **Communion**—You will offer communion during the last session (assuming doing so creates no problems in your church context). Remind the group that taking communion together as believers is significant and unifying in three ways, by:

- proclaiming the Lord's death,
- providing an opportunity for fellowship and unity, and
- giving participants an occasion for remembrance of Jesus.

If there are nonbelievers, explain that communion is for believers. This is a perfect opportunity to ask if they would like to accept Jesus Christ as their Savior and pray the Salvation Prayer on page 37. If they are not ready, then ask them to sit quietly while the believers take communion. Ask someone to read aloud the Scriptures in Matthew 26:26–29 or Luke 22:14–20 and have the group partake of the juice and bread at the appropriate spot in the Scripture reading. Matthew 26:30 says, *"When they had sung a hymn they went out to the Mount of Olives."* Close the time of communion with a worship song.

9. **Fellowship time**—It's important for relationships to develop so group members feel comfortable sharing during discussions. A social time with refreshments provides a nice way to bring closure to the evening and allows time to chat. Encourage everyone to stay. Fellowship is part of the small group experience and allows larger groups to get to know other members.

M&M'S

Use the Session Guide for additional information and help in determining which questions to emphasize during meetings.

Session Guide

Session One—Their Story, page 14

Can You Relate?

● **Have** members bring items to donate to the Salvation Army.

1. **Opening Prayer: Hold** hands as a group and **open** in prayer.

2. **Icebreaker:**

Q: **Ask** each woman to share how Catherine and William Booth (if they were alive today) would use their donated item.

Q: **Ask** for a team to take the donations to your local Salvation Army and report next session how it felt presenting supplies for the "invasion."

3. **Day One: How Does Priscilla and Aquila's Story Relate to Us?, page 17**

Q: **Ask:** Who was familiar with this couple?

Q: **Lead** a discussion of the Scriptures related to Priscilla and Aquila's work, ministry, and mentoring.

◆ **Invite** anyone serving as a couple to describe their service, what they hope to learn from this study, and to offer encouragement to those who aren't serving as a couple.

Q: **Ask** singles what they would like to learn from this study.

4. **Day Two: Priscilla and Aquila Meet Their Mentor, page 20**

Q: **Ask** how Priscilla, Aquila, and Paul's commonalities could attribute to their establishing a working friendship.

Q: **Ask** for experiences of being in a new environment and finding someone with commonalities.

◆ **Discuss** whether it's easier to establish a friendship with Christians.

5. Day Three: Tentmaking, page 23

Q: **Ask** if anyone had heard the term *tentmaking* and discuss the Wikipedia definition.

Q: **Discuss** the trade and legacy of the biblical characters listed:

- Abraham (Answer: wealthy livestock owner—founder/father of Jewish nation)
- Jacob (Answer: shepherd, livestock owner—father of 12 tribes of Israel)
- Joseph (Answer: government official—helped Egypt survive famine)
- David (Answer: harpist, shepherd, king—man after God's own heart, ancestor of Jesus)
- Nehemiah (Answer: cupbearer to the king—rebuilt Jerusalem wall)
- Simon Peter (Answer: fisherman—disciple, preacher for first Christian church)
- Lydia (Answer: businesswoman—first convert and house church in Philippi)
- Luke (Answer: physician—author of Gospel of Luke and Acts)

Q: **Ask:** How did Paul support his missionary work?

Q: **Ask** if anyone knows tentmakers or unpaid church staff. **Discuss** what might motivate these servants and how the group could help them.

6. Day Four: Priscilla and Aquila Mentor a Mentee, page 27

Q: **Ask** someone to read Acts 18:24–28. **Discuss** Priscilla and Aquila's intervention and how Apollos and his audiences benefited.

Q: **Discuss** the dangers of zeal without knowledge.

Q: **Ask** if anyone wants to share an experience similar to Priscilla, Aquila, and Apollos'.

7. Day Five: Where God Leads, We Will Go, page 30

Q: **Ask:** Why would Priscilla and Aquila follow Paul?

◆ **Discuss** God's sovereign plan for Priscilla and Aquila to meet Apollos.

Q: **Ask** for their answers to "location" and "ministry" of Priscilla and Aquila's travels.

Q: **Ask:** How did their willingness to move help the church?

◆ **Ask:** What would each move entail?

Q: **Discuss** answers for the chart of biblical people who followed God's call.

Q: **Ask:** What risks might Priscilla and Aquila encounter befriending Paul?

◆ **Discuss** risks and lifestyle changes involved in following Jesus. **Ask** for a personal testimony.

8. Prayertime (See Leader's Guide, p. 122)

Prayer requests, prayer partner exchange, and group prayer.

9. Fellowship and Refreshments.

Session Two: Maturing in Faith Together, page 34

1. Opening Prayer: Hold hands as a group and **open** in prayer.

2. Icebreaker:

◆ **Have** those who went to the Salvation Army give a report of the experience.

◆ **Invite** several to share their salvation testimony.

3. Day One: Partners in Faith, page 35

Q: **Discuss** personal and shared faith.

Q: **Discuss** the importance of shared faith in partnerships (i.e., marriage, business, investments). **Be sensitive** to anyone unequally yoked and **encourage** them that their life could be a witness to the unbeliever.

◆ **Stress** determining faith before entering into a partnership relationship and discuss ways to accomplish that.

Q: **Read** Jeremiah 15:19*b* and John 17:15–16. **Discuss** the warning in these verses.

Q: **Ask** if anyone prayed the salvation prayer, or would like to pray it now. **Celebrate!**

4. Day Two: Studying God's Word, page 39

Q: **Assign** reading of the Scriptures from Acts and Paul's letters. **Discuss** what Priscilla and Aquila could learn from associating with Paul.

Q: **Read** John 1:1–4; 6:48–51. **Discuss** Jesus as the Incarnation of the Word and why He is the Living Bread.

Q: **Ask:** What is the goal of dieting? What is the result of spiritual dieting?

Q: **Ask:** What is the consequence of starvation? Of spiritual starvation?

◆ **Lead** a discussion on the significance of reading and studying their Bible.

◆ **Discuss** ways to add variety to studying God's Word.

5. Day Three: Praying Continuously, page 42

Q: **Read** Acts 1:13–15; 2:42–47. **Discuss** the prayer and praising of the first Christian believers.

Q: **Personalize** and pray together Acts 4:23–31. **Point out** that the believers were praying Old Testament Scriptures in verses 25–26.

◆ **Discuss** how believers can pray Scripture today.

Q: **Read** Paul's Scriptures regarding prayer. **Discuss** how Priscilla, Aquila, and the group might apply Paul's wisdom to their prayer lives.

Q: **Read** Psalm 134:1. **Discuss** the value of praise.

Q: **Ask** if anyone is uncomfortable praying publicly, or in this group, and **discuss** loving ways to make it easier. **Have** a member personalize and pray Matthew 18:19–20.

Q: **Ask** if anyone would like to share praises. **Remind** them to use their Prayer & Praise Journal.

6. Day Four: Remaining Christ-Centered, page 46

Q: **Compare** Priscilla and Aquila's marriage with that of Sapphira and Ananias, and **discuss** answers to the questions regarding these couples on page 46.

◆ **Discuss** ways to remain personally Christ-centered.

Q: Ask for definitions of a Christ-centered relationship—how to maintain it—and how to make it a witness.

7. Day Five: Sharing Your Testimony, page 49

Q: **Ask** for definitions of a *testimony*. **Read** Psalm 105:1–3; 1 John 5:11.

Q: **Discuss** the chart of biblical characters sharing their testimony and the reception.

Q: **Ask:** What is the value of sharing our story with others?

Q: **Read** 1 Corinthians 2:1–5. **Ask:** How are you encouraged by Paul's inadequacies?

Q: **Read** 1 Peter 3:14–16 aloud together. Ask for a commitment to letting God use their story to help lead others to Him.

8. Prayertime
Prayer requests, prayer partner exchange, and group prayer.

9. Fellowship and Refreshments.

Session Three: Serving Together, page 53

1. Opening Prayer: Hold hands as a group and **open** in prayer.

- **Obtain** blank note cards.
- **Obtain** a whiteboard and marker.

2. Icebreaker:

- ◆ **Hand out** note cards and **instruct** each member to write down a practical way the group could serve together.

- ◆ **Collect** and **shuffle** the cards and **have** someone pick a card and read the idea.

- ◆ **Adopt** this idea as your group project and **discuss** how to put it into action.

3. Day One: An Open Heart and Home, page 54

Q: **Discuss** the use of homes in the early church.

Q: **Discuss** excuses Priscilla could have used to avoid opening her home. **Ask** who uses these excuses and who enjoys hosting church functions.

Q: **Discuss** their responses to the scenario.

Q: **Read** the "hospitality" verses and **ask** if anyone was challenged.

Q: **Discuss** creative ways to use homes for ministry, and **list** answers on a whiteboard. **Ask** who would be willing to try one and **put** her name by it on the board.

4. Day Two: Lay Ministering, page 58

Q: **Determine** if everyone understood the term *lay minister*. **Ask:** How were Priscilla and Aquila lay ministers?

Q: **Read** Ephesians 2:8–10. **Ask:** What work do you think God wants you doing for Him?

Q: **Read** Matthew 28:18–20. **Ask:** What are *all* believers called to do?

Q: **Discuss** the benefits of selfless, payless serving and who set the example.

Q: **Ask** what type of ministry everyone is involved in or would like to be.

5. Day Three: Fellow Workers for Christ, page 62

Q: **Discuss** their definitions of *fellow workers* and how the term applies to Christians.

Q: **Ask:** What happens to the church without unity?

◆ If there was disunity over the icebreaker project, **apply** 1 Corinthians 3:1–8.

Q: **Ask** how married couples could be fellow workers for Christ and **invite** someone to share an experience.

6. Day Four: Allowing God to Use Your Gifts, page 65

Q: **Lead** a discussion of who gives us our gifts and how we are to use them.

Q: **Ask** what gifts they identified in Priscilla and Aquila and how they used them for God.

Q: **Ask:** What gifts has God given each of you and how are you using them for Him?

7. Day Five: Iron Sharpening Iron, page 68

Q: **Ask:** How would Priscilla, Aquila, and Paul benefit spiritually from their close relationship?

Q: **Read** Ephesians 4:11–13. **Ask** which roles they circled and why.

Q: **Ask** someone to read Ecclesiastes 4:9–12. **Discuss** the three-way application.

Q: **Ask** if they feel they are sharpening each other in this group.

◆ **Invite** married members to share how as spouses they spiritually challenge each other.

8. Prayertime

Prayer requests, prayer partner exchange, and group prayer.

9. Fellowship and Refreshments

Session Four: Mentoring Together, page 72

1. Opening Prayer: Hold hands as a group and open in prayer.

2. Icebreaker:

◆ **Have** three people take the roles of Priscilla, Aquila, and Apollos and **act out:**

- Apollos teaching only the baptism of John the Baptist.
- Priscilla and Aquila approaching Apollos and inviting him home.
- The conversation that took place at their home.

3. Day One: Discipling, page 73

Q: **Ask:** How did Priscilla and Aquila disciple Apollos?

Q: **Ask:** How does the Lord refer to new believers or regressing Christians?

Q: **Lead** a discussion of the similarities of a baby's and a baby Christian's maturing process.

Q: **Ask** each member to explain the circumstances of being discipled as a new Christian. If they weren't discipled, what were the consequences and how did they grow spiritually?

Q: **Ask** if anyone wants to share an experience of discipling a new believer.

4. Day Two: Instructing and Correcting, page 76

Q: **Read** Romans 15:14. **Discuss** why believers are equipped to confront.

Q: **Ask:** How did Priscilla and Aquila follow biblical guidelines? (Answer: face-to-face)

Q: **Ask:** Why does God want Christians to instruct or admonish each other and why do we hesitate?

Q: **Read** 2 Timothy 3:14–17 and Psalm 119:11. **Discuss** the importance of memorizing Scripture and how to use a Bible index and concordance.

Q: **Discuss** the corrective approaches used in the Personal Parable on pages 78 and 79.

5. Day Three: Being Sensitive and Receptive, page 80

Q: **Ask:** How did Priscilla and Aquila show sensitivity?

◆ **Discuss** the importance of discretion and timing.

Q: **Assign** the reading of the Proverbs on page 81 and **have** the reader apply the verses to Apollos.

Q: **Discuss** the similarities in Priscilla and Aquila's and Beth's correction techniques.

Q: **Ask:** What do you do if the person isn't receptive to instruction?

Q: **Ask** what they've learned about giving and receiving wise counsel.

6. Day Four: Couples Mentoring, page 85

Q: **Ask:** How does marriage relate to Christ and the church?

◆ **Discuss** ways a Christian marriage can be a good or bad witness.

Q: **Ask**: How do the verses in Titus support couples mentoring couples?

◆ **Lead** a discussion of the value of receiving premarital counseling.

7. Day Five: God Working Through You, page 89

Q: **Ask:** How does God reward those who invest in others' spiritual growth?

Q: **Ask** what rewards Priscilla and Aquila might have received. (Possible answers: the many lives saved through Apollos' evangelism; the gratefulness of other churches; the joy of selfless serving; heavenly crown of glory)

Q: **Discuss** the application of 1 Corinthians 3:6–9*a* to mentoring.

Q: **Invite** some to share when God used others with a similar experience to comfort them, and how they've comforted others.

8. Prayertime

Prayer requests, prayer partner exchange, and group prayer.

9. Fellowship and Refreshments

SESSION FIVE: BALANCING LIFE AND MINISTRY, PAGE 94

- **Obtain:** a complete outfit of clothes, three juggling balls, a balance scale, dried beans, and a bag of M&M's candy.

1. Opening Prayer: Hold hands as a group and **open** in prayer.

2. Icebreaker:

◆ **Let** each member try juggling the balls.

◆ **Use** the dried beans to balance the scale. **Demonstrate** what happens when you add M&M's to one side without taking off any beans.

◆ **Explain** that the dried beans are our daily activities and the M&M's represent something fun and exciting.

◆ Next **remove** enough dried beans from the side opposite the one with M&M's to balance the scale. **Then add** jelly beans, representing ministry opportunities, to that side until the scale is off balance again.

◆ **Discuss** what happens when we continue adding to our life without eliminating anything.

◆ **Enjoy** the remaining M&M's and jelly beans!

3. Day One: Teamwork, page 95

Q: **Ask:** Why do you think Priscilla and Aquila's names are always mentioned together?

Q: **Discuss** names that appear together today and the team's accomplishments, if any.

Q: **Have** someone read 1 Corinthians 12:4–6, 14–22, 25–26. **Discuss** how these verses relate to teamwork, the benefits of working as a team, and the value of every team member.

Q: **Ask:** How does marriage require teamwork?

Q: **Go around** the group **asking** each one to give an answer for the accomplishment of one of the six biblical teams.

Q: **Ask** for testimonies of how teamwork helped balance life and ministry.

4. Day Two: Taking Your Faith to Work, page 99

Q: **Discuss** the world's work versus God's work. **Ask:** Why did God create work?

Q: **Read** Psalm 145:4–6. **Ask:** How and where can we tell of God's mighty works?

Q: **Ask:** How do Paul's teachings help you incorporate working for the Lord into the work you do outside or inside the home?

Q: **Read** Proverbs 16:10–12 (*The Message*). **Ask** for sharing of how being a godly worker displays faith.

5. Day Three: Balancing or Juggling?, page 103

Q: **Ask:** Who takes a day off each week to rest and worship? Why does God want us observing a Sabbath?

Q: **Ask:** Who has trouble saying no? Why?

◆ What are the consequences of saying yes without praying?

Q: **Have** someone read Ephesians 4:22–24. **Ask** for a volunteer model. **Bring out** the complete outfit of clothes. **Advise** the model to put on the new clothes over the old clothes she is wearing. **Lead** a discussion of how this exemplifies not putting off our old ways when we become a Christian and put on new ways.

◆ **Discuss** specific "old ways" to discard and "new ways" to add when becoming a Christian.

Q: **Review** the unbalanced scales from the icebreaker. **Ask** what they've learned about juggling and balancing their life and how they can help each other.

6. Day Four: Prioritizing, page 108

Q: **Read** Matthew 22:36–39. **Ask:** What's a priority to Jesus? (Answer: relationships)

Q: **Have** someone read Isaiah 40:11–12 and **discuss** accomplishments versus relationships.

Q: **Discuss** the results of rating "what they value most" with "where they spend their time and money," and changes they're making to reprioritize relationships and serving.

7. Day Five: A Way of Life, page 112

Q: **Have** someone read 1 Thessalonians 2:4–9, 11–13 and **discuss** how it relates to mentoring.

Q: **Ask** how the story in Mark 14:3–9 encouraged them to do what they can with what they have.

Q: **Ask:** Who knows someone living a life they want to imitate? **Then ask** if it's because of that person's possession and position in life, or because they're living a godly life.

◆ **Discuss** how leading a godly life leads to balancing life and ministry.

8. Prayertime

Review the answers to prayer they have experienced during this study.
Take communion together (see p. 124).
Read the closing prayer on page 119 together.

9. Fellowship and Refreshments

Talk about the study the group wants to do next. **See** page 121 for additional "Face-to-Face" Bible study series.

Prayer & Praise Journal

Prayer & Praise Journal

Prayer & Praise Journal

Prayer & Praise Journal

Prayer & Praise Journal